NIGHT RAIN

ON BAD JOBS AND BAD BOSSES

BY

JERRY GOODWIN

BIFF: Well, I spent six or seven years after high school trying to work myself up. Shipping clerk, salesman, business of one kind or another. And it's a measly manner of existence. To get on that subway on the hot mornings in summer. To devote your whole life to keeping stock, or making phone calls, or selling or buying. To suffer fifty weeks of the year for the sake of a two week vacation, when all you really desire is to be outdoors with your shirt off. And always to have to get ahead of the next fella. And still—that's how you build a future.

Arthur Miller, *Death of a Salesman*

Night Rain: On Bad Jobs and Bad Bosses

© Copyright 2013 by Jerry Goodwin

PREFACE

Bob Dylan's song "The Times They Are A Changin'" was a definitive song of the 1960's and expressed the hope and optimism of that decade.

I grew up in the 1960's, came of age in the 1970's, settled into life in the 1980's, went through a transition in the 1990's, and have struggled in the millennial generation.

This is a work memoir and it won't take you long to discover I've had some pretty horrible jobs. I've done lots of things: working at McDonald's, working with a sign painter, working in the loan departments of savings and loans, working for a commuter airline, working for a Mexican foods manufacturer, and working in the insurance inspections business. I was a temporary employee on three different occasions.

I think frequently of the line from the Robert Frost poem about the road not taken. When I was in high school my major focus was on the end of the world. I was a Jehovah's Witness and I didn't make long term plans because I was certain the world as I knew it wouldn't exist much longer. Life for me and other Jehovah's Witnesses took on a temporary quality.

You didn't go to college. You didn't plan on a career. The organization preferred that you not get married or have children. Everything should be devoted to the "Kingdom ministry," preaching the "good news" that a new world order was coming quickly on the horizon.

The year 1975 was our focus back then. The Watchtower Society had published a chronology that purported to prove that 6,000 years of human existence was coming to an end and we were about to enter a "millennial day" when Jesus Christ would rule over a paradise earth. I saw significance in every major world event because it pointed to the fulfillment of Bible prophecy.

This memoir is being written in 2013 and Armageddon hasn't happened yet. I left Jehovah's Witnesses back in 1976, but it wasn't because Armageddon didn't come.

I don't think the temporary view of things ever left me. I took jobs that didn't excite me because I had to have a job and I could theoretically keep looking for something better. But I found myself staying for years, living day to day.

There were the things that interested me. There was baseball and football and basketball. There were books. There was music. There was always the dream of being a writer.

I have no way of knowing how things might have been different if I had taken a different road. If I had gone to college, I might have wound up a journalist. I might have loved my career, but I might have found myself burned out and disillusioned. All I can talk about is the way things really happened.

I will admit to some anger over how I've been treated in some jobs. I subscribed to the motto the late Al Davis, owner of the Oakland Raiders, coined: "commitment to excellence." I've always wanted to excel at whatever job I did.

What employers have demanded more and more over the years is production. Even office work has similarities to an assembly line. You aren't measured as much by the quality—the craftsmanship if you will—of your work as by the volume. It isn't in my nature to produce shoddy work.

I'm sure there are worse things than having a job you hate. But having a job you hate (with good reason in most cases) diminishes the quality of your life. I have never been able to turn off the "job button." It was with me at home, in my sleep, and on my weekends (if I was lucky enough to get a weekend). When I was doing some of these jobs I felt almost sick on my way to work and there was really no light at the end of the tunnel.

When you say you hate your job some people automatically respond, "Be glad you have a job" or they'll offer the seemingly obvious solution to find another job.

When people tell you how grateful you should be to have a bad job I think of slaves on plantations. "Don't complain about your chains. You have a roof over your head and food to eat."

Finding another job isn't always easy either. There aren't enough jobs for all the people looking for jobs. There are often hurdles you can't surmount when you look for another job. You may not have the experience they want. They may not like the way you look. You may be too old or too young or too whatever. There is a lot to job hunting that is not obvious.

I also resent the implication that somehow giving you a job is doing you a favor. The employer benefits more from the arrangement than the employee. Profits come from the money left after expenses paid by the employer. Employees produce more value than they get compensated and that is where the employer's profits come from.

But a discussion of the inadequacy of the United States economy is not the purpose of this memoir. I might consider that in a future book.

I apologize for arcane details about some of these jobs, but I feel they are necessary for the story.

I want to acknowledge some of the people who have been important to me. There is obviously my Mom. Her kindness and generosity are a true inspiration. My late brother Gary and my cousin Opie were my best friends as I grew up. My grandparents were hard-working, kind, and decent people who deserved much better than they received. My aunt Ruby was most of the most generous and compassionate people I ever knew. I want to thank my brother John. Friends I have met in my work life, such as Beverly and Janet and others, have been inspirational to me. I want to thank Pat, Valerie, and Deborah for their friendship. Now, as Jackie Gleason used say, "Awaaaay we go!"

ARKANSAS DAYS

When I was young I lived for a time with my grandparents, Opie and Clara Stinson, in Winfield, Arkansas. Winfield was a rural area located outside of Waldron, the County Seat of Scott County, Arkansas.

We lived on a farm that my grandparents rented. They had a cow for milk, raised a hog for slaughter, and had chickens for eggs and for meat.

We lived in an old rundown clapboard house with a porch that wrapped around three sides. The only modern convenience was electricity. We didn't have running water and the bathroom was an outhouse down a rocky trail.

Our water came from a well and we drank from a common dipper.

I don't know how my grandparents met. I know that my grandmother developed a major antipathy toward my grandfather's relatives in Heavener, Oklahoma. When they had an argument she invariably mentioned Heavener. You had the feeling that Heavener was the equivalent of the fire pits of Hell itself.

My Uncle Clyde and his wife Elizabeth and their children Jimmy and Linda lived just up the road. Linda was a constant companion to me and my brother Gary while we lived in Winfield. She was the prototypical tomboy.

My brother Gary, who was two years younger than me, and I moved in with our grandparents after my mother and father divorced. My mother subsequently married a man my grandmother didn't like. My mother and stepfather lived in Booneville, about a forty-five minute drive from Waldron, and I usually saw her about once a week when she came up on her day off.

My mother and stepfather both worked at the State Tuberculosis Sanatorium outside of Booneville. It was commonly referred to as "The Hill" because of the terrain where it was built.

Winfield was located on a rocky dirt road that became almost impassable in the winter with snow and rain. My grandparents didn't drive and didn't have a car. We got our groceries from a store in Waldron. My Uncle Clyde drove my grandfather, who was equipped with a grocery list written by my grandmother, into town when they got their Social Security checks. They would pay the previous balance and then start anew.

I always looked forward to the grocery trips. My grandmother bought bottles of Coca Cola, vanilla ice cream, Milky Way bars, and bubble gum for Gary and me at the start of every month.

There were several outbuildings on the property. A smokehouse was at the rear of the house, a chicken house on the left side, and then a barn. The outbuildings all had tin roofs and I liked the sound of rain on the tin roofs at night. I could pull the covers up and I felt safe and warm and secure.

Summers were the best time. My grandparents were early risers, both by habit and by necessity. But I got to sleep late when I got out of school. My grandmother saved breakfast for me. She made wonderful biscuits and gravy. After breakfast, Gary and I got to play with Linda, whose imagination was boundless.

Our imaginary heroes were usually anti-establishment. We pretended we were outlaws like Jesse James or Billy the Kid or soldiers in the Confederate army.

Arkansas seceded from the Union and joined the Confederacy in the Civil War.

Linda also got me interested in baseball. We didn't have any equipment except for a ball and a stick that we used for a bat. She became a fan of a first baseman named Jim Gentile of the Baltimore Orioles and so did I. I've remained an Orioles fan ever since.

Arkansas summers are hot and smothering wet with humidity. In the afternoons the heat lay in layers over the pine and cedar trees. Mud dauber wasps buzzed around building their nests and you could occasionally hear mockingbirds in the trees. You had to be wary of copperhead snakes and water moccasins. Chiggers and ticks were eager to devour your blood. Dog ticks, big, gray, bulbous monsters were particularly bad. Sometimes it took turpentine and tweezers to extract ticks embedded in your skin.

My grandparents were always busy. My grandmother grew a garden and we got the benefits of fresh tomatoes, fried potatoes, fried okra, and cornbread for supper. Pinto beans were a frequent main course and there is nothing finer than pinto beans and hot cornbread.

They slopped the hog and milked the cow and fed the chickens and collected eggs. My grandfather put fruit on the roof of the chicken house to dry in the sun. My grandmother canned vegetables and fruits as the summer wore on.

I particularly liked it when she canned sauerkraut. She chopped the cabbage until it was very fine and put the cabbage into a briny mix and I would take handfuls of the salted cabbage out and eat it.

When she wasn't working my grandmother read magazines like "True Story." The stories weren't true at all, of course, but fictional "tell all" accounts of romance gone bad. She liked a soap opera called "Love of Life." In prime time television she liked "Perry Mason" and "Gunsmoke."

Other shows I remember from that period were "The Andy Griffith Show" and "The Dick Van Dyke Show" and "My Favorite Martian." Saturday morning shows like "Rocky and Bullwinkle" or "Underdog" or "Sky King" come to mind.

I remember shows like Art Linkletter and "The Ed Sullivan Show."

The national news we watched was the "Huntley-Brinkley" report on NBC.

My grandmother got mail from her kids living in California and New Mexico. My Uncle Fred and his family lived in Corcoran, California. My Aunt Hattie and her family also lived in Corcoran. My Aunt Erma Jean and her family lived in New Mexico. My grandmother wrote letters by hand with a fountain pen. I wish I knew what happened to her fountain pen.

A big oak tree grew near the road and my grandfather put a swing in the oak tree. I liked to swing and to try to reach higher and higher. One time the County was working on the road and they left a road grader parked under the tree. I liked the scent of freshly turned earth. I remember my cousin Jimmy, who liked working on cars, suspended an engine from the oak tree one time.

We got occasional visits from relatives. My grandmother's sister Bertha lived in Oklahoma and she and her husband came for visits. My grandmother was concerned about appearances and

Gary and I were instructed to be on our best behavior for Bertha's visits. We were also led to believe that Bertha and her husband were affluent and that Butler, Oklahoma, where they lived, was an upscale community.

My aunt Erma Jean and her family came for a few days every summer. Gary and I got excluded from most activities and even Linda hung out with the Button family. I remember my grandmother buying a case of Coca-Cola one time that we kept hidden until the Button family returned to New Mexico and I never enjoyed Coke more than that day.

Another time my grandmother's brother Clarence and his wife visited from Bakersfield, California. He set up a slide projector and showed slides of his house in Bakersfield. California seemed beautiful and exotic.

It wasn't unusual for even young boys to have pocket knives and I had a pocket knife. One day I was whittling and the knife slipped and cut my left thumb. I still have the scar.

My grandmother collected green stamps and she offered to get me a watch with green stamps. My Uncle Clyde would pick it up when it was available. I remember waiting expectantly several times before I finally got the watch. I was thrilled. I wish I knew what became of that watch.

I struggled some with school. It meant getting up in the dark and having my grandmother give me the equivalent of a sponge bath. A full bath meant drawing water from the well and heating the water and taking a bath in a wash tub. It wasn't practical to do every day.

But I didn't have to worry about that during the summer. In the evenings my grandparents washed their feet and sat out on the front porch. Fireflies darted here and there and we tried our best to keep cool.

One time Gary and I were sword fighting with sharp sticks. He didn't parry my attack and the stick struck him below the right eye. I still shudder when I think I could have blinded him.

I finished the first grade in Waldron and as the start of the new school year approached my mother and stepfather came to take Gary and me to buy new clothes. But instead of buying clothes in Waldron they took us to Booneville and it was quickly apparent they weren't going to take us back home.

I went to Booneville elementary school for the second grade and we lived with my stepfather's parents. I didn't like either of them, but particularly disliked his mother. She was one of those people who acted syrupy sweet around other people and was cold and abusive in private. She never went really overboard in physical abuse, but I thought even spanking was inappropriate. When I related how I was treated to my grandmother she was enraged.

My mother, stepfather, Gary, and my brother John, who was born in 1960, eventually moved to a house independent of my stepfather's parents. I remember waking up one school day too late for breakfast and my mother giving me some cookies to take with me on the bus. I remember a kid on the bus telling me the advantage of cursive writing over printing. Cursive writing was faster.

I got bullied in school. Someone had concocted the name "Timbutter" for me. I don't know what it meant, but it sounded derogatory. One day on the playground I was enraged enough to start throwing rocks at the bullies. I threw low toward their feet and didn't do any real damage. I got sent back to the classroom.

One morning while I was riding the bus to school I saw a banged up Chevy being towed. It looked like the one my Mom drove. When I got home that afternoon I learned she had been in an accident that morning.

The second grade boys liked to play with toy pistols and I really wanted a pistol. My mother finally bought me one.

My Mom usually drove Gary, John, and me to her in-laws when she went to work. Around Christmas I remember seeing the strings of bright-colored holiday lights on the houses in the early morning dark. One morning the car got stuck on the dirt road and we had to walk back home.

As the school year approached for third grade for me and first grade for Gary, my mother asked if we would like to live with our grandparents again. I guess our unhappiness was palpable. We eagerly said yes and moved back to Winfield.

Gary and I had to deal with bullies on the school bus. Some of the older boys liked to "flip" your ears with rings they wore on their fingers. On one occasion they even threw lighted firecrackers on the bus.

I had to deal with asthma. I fought and fought for breath. The one good thing about having asthma was getting to watch the entire 1963 World Series between the Yankees and Dodgers. I stayed home from school and I saw Sandy Koufax pitch game one and overpower the Yankees and that started a Dodger sweep of the Yankees.

Music I remember from those days includes LeRoy Van Dyke and Johnny Horton. LeRoy Van Dyke recorded a song called "Walk on By" with a distinctive guitar line. Johnny Horton recorded songs like "All For the Love of a Girl" and "North to Alaska" and there was poignancy in Johnny Horton's music because he died young in a car crash.

When winter came we had to use a wood stove to heat the kitchen. One year the flue got blocked and smoke filled the house. We had the choice of staying inside with the smoke or going outside into sub-freezing weather.

I remember putting pieces of plastic on the wood stove top so I could see the plastic melt.

Going to bed was an adventure. We had a feather bed, but until you were in bed a while and your body heat warmed the bed it was like jumping onto a big block of ice. So I would take a deep breath and plunge into the feathery depth of the bed and wait to get warm.

We didn't go to church much, but we went on occasion. One Sunday my grandparents hosted the pastor of the

Baptist church and his family. He had some really tall sons. We were playing a form of keep away with a ball in the living room. I tried to get the ball over their heads and smashed the light bulb.

I looked forward to Christmas, especially when I still believed in Santa Claus. One year I wanted to hide out in the pantry in the kitchen and await the visit of Santa Claus. I got talked out of it and went on believing in Santa Claus a little while longer.

We were surrounded by pine and cedar forest and we cut our own Christmas tree every year. My grandfather cut down the tree and we dragged it back to the house and draped colored lights around the branches. I loved the resin scent of pine or cedar.

The best gift I got during those years was a bicycle. I used the training wheels for a time and finally one day in frustration took off the training wheels and found I could ride without them. Gary never learned, or didn't care to learn, to ride a bike, but Linda and I rode together.

As winter came on we looked for the first snow. It invariably meant power outages and it meant school would be closed. We would watch the snow sifting down from the sky like granulated sugar and carpeting the trees and roofs and ground. Then my grandfather took a clean container and gathered snow to make snow ice cream.

My grandmother added sugar, milk, eggs, and vanilla extract to the snow to make the snow ice cream.

I collected baseball cards back then. I got most of my cards from packs of bubble gum, but I remember Jello had baseball cards on their boxes and I got some cards thanks to Jello.

Before they rented the farm, my grandparents owned some property that became known as the "old place." Every now and then Gary and I went walking with our grandfather up the rocky road that cut through the pine and cedar trees to the old place. We collected nuts we called English walnuts and sometimes my grandfather went hunting for squirrels.

It's hard to believe now that I ate fried squirrel, but at the time it seemed normal and the squirrel tasted good. After my grandfather shot the squirrels, he would skin and dress the meat and my grandmother fried it.

My grandmother began to experience health problems. I remember her lying in bed in the freezing cold bedroom. Waldron's town doctor, Doctor Wright, actually made house calls. My grandmother weathered the first serious health crisis, but it was the harbinger of things to come.

I didn't have any confidence in my athletic ability. When we played baseball in school someone would hit for me and I would be the base runner. I always loved sports, but never felt confident playing any sports.

I was in a fifth grade classroom in Waldron on November 22, 1963, when a teacher came to tell us that President Kennedy had been shot. My thoughts immediately flashed to the name Lyndon Baines Johnson. Later on, I learned that President Kennedy had been killed. That night I watched the television news coverage of Air Force One landing at Andrews Air Force Base and saw President Kennedy's coffin put on a lift and taken from the airplane and put into a hearse. I saw Jackie Kennedy and

Robert Kennedy get into the hearse to accompany the President's body.

President Johnson gave a brief speech asking for the help of the American people and God.

I was watching TV when Jack Ruby shot Lee Harvey Oswald in the Dallas Police Department garage and I learned later that Oswald had died.

Then there was the funeral for President Kennedy and watching the black horse with no rider and the lighting of the eternal flame at Arlington National Cemetery.

My grandmother got seriously ill in March of 1964 and went into the hospital in Waldron. Children weren't allowed to visit inside the hospital and I stood outside the window of the room where my grandmother was staying. She wasn't aware I was there and I tapped lightly on the window until I saw my aunt Elizabeth shaking her head in disapproval. Then my grandmother died and my life changed.

It had been a few happy years in my personal life while world events were in turmoil. Television news shows started covering events in a faraway place called Vietnam. The Berlin Wall was constructed. The civil rights movement began in earnest and civil rights workers were abused or murdered. We experienced the Cuban Missile Crisis in October, 1962. I went to bed at night wondering if I would die in a missile attack overnight.

The weekend President Kennedy was assassinated my brother John swallowed some medications and was seriously ill, but I didn't know at the time. We didn't have a phone in Winfield and he battled for his life without my knowledge.

But John survived and a few months later Gary and I were living with him, my stepfather, and Mom near Booneville.

It must have been about 1962 or 1963 that I became a football fan. I saw a cigarette advertisement for a book you could buy about the NFL. Technically, it required sending something from cigarette packs along with the money to buy the book. I sent a letter explaining why I didn't have the cigarette pack items and they sent me the book anyway.

I remember a long article about Fran Tarkenton of the Minnesota Vikings. Tarkenton was known for his scrambling ability when he was under pressure and the passing pocket broke down. For some reason, Linda, Gary, and I became fans of the New York Giants and quarterback Y. A. Tittle. I was crushed when the Giants lost the 1963 NFL championship game to the Chicago Bears.

The day of my grandmother's funeral was appropriately gray and rainy. I had gone one time with my grandmother to the cemetery and the talk turned to souls. I couldn't quite grasp the concept of the soul. I asked her, "But is the soul *you*?"

Now, as far as I knew, my grandmother's soul was in heaven and Gary and I moved to the "state house" my Mom and stepfather occupied.

The house was called a "state house" because it was owned by the State of Arkansas, not because it was elaborate. It came as part of my Mom's job at the Sanatorium.

Gary and I started to school in Booneville and we caught the school bus down by the highway. The bus was usually so crowded that I wound up standing on the way to school. These days it would be illegal to have a kid stand in the aisle, but that was the way it was back then.

MOVE TO CALIFORNIA

Arkansas has long been one of the poorest states in the union and my Mom and stepfather decided it was time to move to the more prosperous state of California. In April, 1965, we packed up some possessions in an old Ford Falcon and started to California.

We had car trouble in Oklahoma and finally got to see where my grandmother's sister Bertha lived. Butler didn't quite live up to expectations. It was just a typical small Oklahoma town and Bertha lived in a nice, but not extraordinary house. We spent one night and got the car repaired and headed on to California.

We went to Corcoran. It's an agricultural town in central California surrounded by cotton fields. The J. G. Boswell Company was the major employer and they employed my Uncle Fred and we stayed for a few days at his house.

It didn't take long for things to get too crowded at my Uncle Fred's place, so we took a dingy small apartment while my stepfather looked for work. He got a job with a man named Frank Toste outside of Fresno.

Toste owned a dairy called Hillview Dairy Farm at Manning and Marks Avenue outside of Fresno. I don't know why it was called "Hillview" because it was on flat land and surrounded by Thompson seedless grape vineyards. The closest town was Caruthers and American Union Elementary School was the closest school.

Toste provided a house and a daily free gallon of milk as perks of the job and we moved into the small house at 9074 S. Marks. Gary, John, and I shared a room. Gary and John had a bunk bed and I slept on a conventional bed.

I remember the sweet scent of honeysuckle. A honeysuckle vine grew outside the house.

When I first went to American Union I was immediately intimidated. I saw some calculations on the blackboard that looked totally unfamiliar to me. Then I found out that the classroom was shared by the fifth and sixth grades and the work on the blackboard was for the upper grade.

I immediately stood out as different. I had a Southern accent from having lived in Arkansas. I also had a short Marine style haircut. My Mom had begun cutting our hair to save money and a short haircut was the easiest for her to manage.

We did our major grocery shopping at Mr. G's Country Store in Caruthers. Gary and I became fans of the comic book section and especially of the Marvel

Comics Group that included "The Fantastic Four" and "Spider-Man." Comic books were 12 cents each. Mr. G's had a small paperback book section and I grew increasingly fond of checking the books too.

Caruthers had a fast food place called The Walk Up that had really good hamburgers and frozen Pepsis. You got Pepsis in glass bottles back then and they simply put the bottles into the freezer. They were like an early version of a slushie, but better.

Frank Toste expanded his operations and he built several new houses for his employees. We moved to the house at 9098 S. Marks. There was no lawn and the ground was covered by puncture vines, so-called "Goat Head" stickers. Gary and I spent hours pulling the vines out by hand.

I had my own room at the new house. Gary and John shared a room. I was starting to collect books and I put some on the window sill. I didn't think it would be a problem, but Frank Toste's wife complained that the window wasn't "book shelves," so I took them down.

The new house had a crawlspace and I thought it would be good to have something like the Bat Cave beneath the home. I fantasized about being a super hero like Spider-Man going from roof top to roof top and fighting crime and I thought my own version of the Bat Cave would be a good headquarters.

We probably made our first trip to Modesto around May or June to visit my aunt Ruby and cousin Opie. The median areas of Highway 99 were bright with oleander bushes and the trip to Modesto started a life change for Gary and me.

I had met my cousin Opie before when he and his family lived in Arkansas. For a time Opie and my aunt Ruby even lived with my grandparents. But I never really knew Opie until we moved to California.

Opie was confined to a wheelchair because of arthritis. He had very limited mobility in his legs and arms. He couldn't move his head at all. But he had a strong passion for life and for the things he believed in.

We immediately connected on interests such as sports and country music. Opie borrowed albums from his sister-in-law Delaine Edwards and recorded them. In the early days he recorded albums on open reel tape and through a microphone. He later discovered so-called "patch cords" that provided much better recordings without the noise that came from using a microphone.

Opie and my aunt Ruby were two of the most generous people I ever knew. They didn't have much materially, but they never hesitated in sharing what they had. As a kid, I didn't truly appreciate just how poor they were. I always felt richer when I was in Modesto because I could finally relax and Opie was always generous with Pepsis. Having abundant Pepsis felt like being rich to me.

Ruby had been widowed for many years by the time we moved to California. She had three other sons in addition to Opie: my cousin Bob, my cousin Thurman, and my cousin Elmer. Elmer hated his name and didn't use it. For years, he had been called "Duck," which evolved into the name "Doug."

When we first moved to California Bob and Thurman had left home and were married and had children. Doug was still single and thinking about his next big career move, which turned out to be joining the California Highway Patrol.

I remember the drop down desk Opie had in the living room and the portable typewriter he had in the bedroom. I remember the scent of Lemon Pledge that he used to clean the furniture in the living room. I can recall the scent of coffee brewing in the morning. Opie had a big cup that he used and he drank coffee through a straw.

Opie kept a stick with rubber bands wrapped around it to use as a tool for helping him pick up things, eat, and so on. At some point we started playing a version of baseball using a ping pong ball and Opie used his stick as a bat. He batted left handed and he got credit for hits and runs if Gary and I couldn't field the ball properly.

Opie taught me the moves to play chess. He liked to play head games with you when you played. He would say something like, "Are you sure you want to do that?" He and his friend Roy Shaw used to play. Opie always made sure to break off the cross on the top of the king chess piece because he felt the cross was a symbol of false religion.

The biggest thing in Opie's life was being a Jehovah's Witness. Witnesses commonly refer to themselves as being "in the truth." Being a Witness is a full time job. They had five meetings a week on three different days. You were expected to devote at least 10 hours a month to the "field service" or "field ministry," which involved going door to door or conducting Bible studies based on Watchtower Society publications.

Back then Opie did his field service time by writing letters. He got a magazine that published letters with addresses of the senders and he wrote them letters about Jehovah's Witnesses beliefs.

As we spent time together Opie began to indoctrinate Gary and me into Witness beliefs. I think the biggest game changer was the publication of a book called *Life Everlasting in Freedom of the Sons of God* by the Watchtower Society in 1966.

The book showed a chronology that suggested Armageddon, the end of "the present system of things," would occur no later than the fall of 1975. The book made a rather elaborate argument about millennial days and a millennial Sabbath. I was only thirteen years old, but I thought Jehovah's Witnesses had an impressive way of backing up what they said from the Bible and I believed in the Bible implicitly.

The first major step I made toward becoming a Witness was to stop saluting the flag in school. Opie subscribed to the *Watchtower* and *Awake!* magazines for me, and Gary and I were eventually contacted for a Bible study by a guy named John Shubin, who was a member of the Fresno South Congregation of Jehovah's Witnesses.

John worked as a "pioneer" for Jehovah's Witnesses. Pioneers devoted a minimum of 100 hours a month to the door-to-door ministry and to conducting Bible studies. On top of that, they attended the five weekly meetings and performed duties at the Kingdom Hall.

The car John drove was an old black VW Beetle. He had lost the ignition key and he used a kitchen butter knife to start the car. He was almost always low on gas and tapped the "reserve" tank. One time Gary and I were out with him in the field ministry when he ran out of gas and we pushed the car to the nearest gas station. John got sick from the exertion and threw up in the bathroom.

When you went door to door in the field ministry you tried to find an article in one of the magazines, usually *Awake!* to talk about. Many Witnesses would introduce themselves as "Bible students" who were out talking to friends and neighbors about conditions in the world and about God's promise to establish a new earth.

A friend I made in the congregation was Tommy Zurita. Tommy had a pretty wife named Diana and two young children. He worked for a grocery store. Tommy liked sports. He had played basketball at Washington Union High School, where Gary and I both attended. One problem I consistently had with Witnesses was their limited knowledge of what was going on in the world. Their world was limited to meetings and whatever they read in the Watchtower publications and it was refreshing to know someone who knew something of the "world."

Things progressed and Gary and I got more involved. I remember John Shubin taking us to a small town called Fowler near Fresno where I made my first magazine placement. John knew from previous visits that this person was likely to take the magazines. Magazine placements, book placements, and Bible studies were among the statistics kept by the Watchtower Society.

Gary and I joined the Theocratic Ministry School. You were assigned a topic and you prepared a short presentation to deliver before the congregation. Women weren't allowed to appear alone. Their "talks" were conversations with another woman, but male members gave solo presentations.

I have never liked public speaking and I always found giving talks an excruciating experience.

Gary and I went with John Shubin to the Bakersfield District Assembly in 1968 and we were baptized there. We were persuaded to volunteer and went to work in a snow cone stand. A guy falsely accused Gary of stabbing him with an ice pick and we didn't go back.

In the weeks before an assembly the local congregations arranged for housing for Witnesses who didn't have much money. Gary, John, and I stayed in a travel trailer that was on the ground. The morning we were getting ready to return to Fresno John accused Gary and me of being too noisy. He also said there would be no restroom stops on the way.

Gary and I were getting an introduction to the authoritarianism that was part of being a Jehovah's Witness.

I recall a trip we took by chartered bus to Anaheim to see Nathan H. Knorr give a talk in Anaheim Stadium, where the California Angels played. Knorr was president of the Watchtower Society and a member of the Governing Body. He was also one of the 144,000 that Jehovah's Witnesses said would inhabit heaven with

Christ. We second tier people would remain on earth.

My Mom gave Gary and me money to fund the trip and I remember she sent along some split pea soup for us to eat. We were sitting in seats in the middle of the bus when a guy named William Burdine, who was the "congregation servant," essentially ordered us to the back of the bus so he and his wife could have our seats.

I don't remember any real details of Knorr's talk. The day was gray and the air was scented by smog. Knorr probably had the usual talking points about the end of the world being upon us. I was already getting disenchanted with being a Jehovah's Witness.

You were considered "strong in the truth" when you attended all five weekly meetings and put in your ten hours every month in the field ministry. You also couldn't have much interest in anything outside the organization of Jehovah's Witnesses. You were considered "worldly" if you talked about other things.

I had the fortune, or misfortune, of being a pretty good student. The expectation was that a good student would go on to college and pursue a professional career. But Jehovah's Witnesses strongly discouraged college. We were told "the time was short" and it was pointless to go to college because we would never be able to pursue a career anyway. Marriage was also discouraged.

The Apostle Paul had written that staying single allowed you to better serve God.

In 1969 our expectations were high. My Mom and stepfather purchased a used Ford Falcon. Opie was convinced it was Jehovah acting to get us transportation to go the District Assembly in Los Angeles. The assembly was to be held at Dodger Stadium.

I was learning to drive then and I drove part of the way to Los Angeles. Roy Shaw did most of the driving. On the way to Los Angeles I saw a car with the Tetragrammaton on the rear windshield. The Tetragrammaton is the Hebrew representation of God's name. No vowels were used and the best guess we have is "Jehovah" or "Yahweh."

We were offered accommodations with a Witness family and it was a major improvement over the camper Gary and I stayed in during the Bakersfield assembly. Opie was the navigator in Los Angeles and he and Roy Shaw bickered over directions to and from Dodger Stadium.

Opie began to have problems on the first day of the assembly. People in wheelchairs were usually assigned to a specific area to watch the program. But Opie kept getting moved to areas where he couldn't see or hear the program, supposedly because of fire department regulations. Finally, after about a day and a half we decided to return home.

On the way home the Falcon we were driving started making a loud noise. I think it was probably the muffler.

In the late 1960's radio station KMAK changed its format to country and my family and I became KMAK fans. I liked all their disc jockeys, but especially a guy named Gary Dee. Gary Dee roared onto the air and called himself "Fearless Nighttime." He was funny and outrageous and talked about how his cerebrum was attacked by his cerebellum. But he began more and more to attack people on welfare.

Opie was extremely sensitive about criticism of people on welfare. When I was in the eleventh grade I had a teacher named John Castle. Mr. Castle tended to expound more on his right-wing political views than to actually teach American history. But Mr. Castle convinced me of the evils of "socialism" and that included social safety net programs that my aunt Ruby and Opie used.

Opie and I got into a rip-roaring argument one day about the alleged socialism of social programs. I've since totally changed my views, of course.

Another big argument I had with Opie was over the Kent State shootings. I'm convinced even now that the National Guard overreacted and essentially murdered the students they fired upon. Opie was fairly right-wing on law enforcement issues and he defended the National Guard.

I wanted to be a disc jockey when I got out of high school. I listened to people like Gary Dee and I occasionally pretended I was on the air and announce "The Jerry Goodwin Show."

I don't recall when I wrote the Watchtower Society to ask if there would be a conflict in being a disc jockey and my Witness beliefs. Disc jockeys have to read political announcements, for instance, or play the National Anthem and that goes contrary to Witness beliefs. My rationale was that it wasn't me personally doing these things, but just acting as an employee of the radio station. But the Watchtower Society essentially said I couldn't be a disc jockey without violating Witness beliefs.

So being a Jehovah's Witness had a major impact on all areas of my life. I had to worry about not standing for the National Anthem, or not getting a blood transfusion if I got injured, or possibly going to prison if I refused the military draft. I had no true career options except for pursuing the Jehovah's Witness ministry.

It really didn't take long for me to begin getting disenchanted with Jehovah's Witnesses. The constant control and restrictions began to grate on me. I didn't like going out door-to-door, for instance. One Saturday morning my friend Tommy Zurita essentially rousted me awake to go out in the field ministry.

I think it was about the time he was in the eighth grade that Gary developed an interest in stereo equipment and music. His teacher, a guy named Gary Edwards, gave him a phonograph. When he started working Gary began acquiring stereo equipment ranging from an eight track player to an open reel tape recorder.

Gary also started to acquire a music collection. He was a major Buck Owens fan and he became very fond of a live album Buck Owens recorded in London, England. As much as I liked Buck Owens and Don Rich, I got pretty tired of hearing their live version of "Johnny B. Goode."

I was part of the Class of '71 at Washington Union High School in Easton.

Some people who attended my elementary school got transfers to the high school in Caruthers because Washington Union had a significant African-American student body.

I never had any significant problems with the African-American students, although I was amazed at the ability of some kids to say so many four letter or profane words in such a short time. African-American kids could out-cuss any white kid any day.

At Washington Union they had different courses of study depending on your goals. If you intended to attend college, you took college prep courses. If you were looking for a business career, you took business courses. I started off in the college prep program, but switched to business because Jehovah's Witnesses were always preaching the evils of college.

In 1967 I traveled with my family on vacation to Arkansas. I met my stepfather's sister Edith Lane and her daughter LoAnna, who was the first love of my life. LoAnna had beautiful long raven black hair and I liked her bold, impetuous personality.

Edith and her family were living in a mobile home while her husband A. D. was off in military service. A. D. was a career military man.

The song "Honey" by Bobby Goldsboro was on the charts then and it reinforced my sadness when we traveled back to California and I couldn't spend time with LoAnna.

1968 had rapid fire events. The Tet Offensive in Vietnam showed that the war was far from over, despite the claims of the U. S. military. Senator Eugene McCarthy made a surprisingly strong showing against President Johnson in the New Hampshire primary. President Johnson announced he would not seek reelection. Senator Robert Kennedy then entered the race and got accused by McCarthy supporters of being a carpetbagger, allegedly letting McCarthy take the risks while Kennedy sat on the sidelines.

In April, 1968, my stepfather's father died and we went to Arkansas for the funeral. I was really happy to see LoAnna again. It turned out it was the last time I saw her.

As a Jehovah's Witness, I wasn't supposed to be interested in politics, but I was rooting for Robert Kennedy to become the next president. Kennedy had entered the race late and it was a scramble to get his campaign organized. He became the first Kennedy to lose a primary when he lost in Oregon and it was crucial to win the California primary.

The primary was on June 4. Kennedy made a whistle stop tour through the San Joaquin Valley on May 30. I went with my Mom and brothers to the train station and we waited for Kennedy to arrive. Two nuns were dressed in full habits and standing in front of us. They were excited when the train pulled in and the caboose, where Kennedy would speak, was right in front of us.

A guy who looked like a college student was holding up a sign supporting Eugene McCarthy and an African-American kid came over, snatched the sign away, and ripped it in half.

There were no high roof tops in the train station, but I had an uneasy feeling as I stood there. I could imagine some cruel man with a gun. Just a few days later Sirhan-Sirhan shot Robert Kennedy in the Ambassador Hotel in Los Angeles and Kennedy died the next day.

In the following days I remember watching the funeral train's progress on television and hearing Ted Kennedy's eloquent eulogy to his brother before Robert Kennedy was buried at Arlington National Cemetery.

Just weeks before Robert Kennedy was killed Martin Luther King was assassinated in Memphis, Tennessee, where he had gone to lend support to striking garbage workers. Reverend King was the foremost civil rights leader in the country and his murder was devastating to everyone hoping for peaceful progress on civil rights.

But as a Jehovah's Witness I saw all these events as proof of the "end times" prophesied in the Bible. When I think back now I wonder how I could have been so enthusiastic. Armageddon, according to Witness belief, will kill almost everyone on the planet. That would include friends and family members who happen not to be Jehovah's Witnesses.

My life became a mix of being a Jehovah's Witness and a student at Washington Union High School in Easton, California. Washington Union was a relatively small school, but high school was exciting in some ways. It meant having sports teams to root for and listening to rock and roll music on the school bus and buying lunch at the Panther Patio.

The Panther Patio was a snack bar with an open patio area attached to it.

My usual lunch was a ham and cheese sandwich and a cup of Pepsi. Lots of times I went to my afternoon classes still hungry.

A guy named Richard Gabel became my major nemesis in high school. Gabel had gone to American Union Elementary School too, but in high school he turned into a bully. He was smart and a gifted athlete. In high school he grew his hair long and around his shoulders.

Gabel thought it was clever to call me "Goober." I don't know if it was after the character in "The Andy Griffith Show" or if it was just a generic term for someone from the south.

I had problems with locking my first locker at Washington Union, so I brought a combination lock. Gabel must have watched over my shoulder and memorized the combination. I came back to find the lock turned around and locked.

I probably didn't help my nerd image by buying a briefcase to carry my books. But I got tired of constantly dropping books and papers and a briefcase seemed like a practical and classy solution.

The briefcase idea also came from my Witness experience. We carried bags with copies of *The Watchtower* and *Awake* magazines or Watchtower books or the Bible. We referred to our bags as "book bags."

I developed friendships with Robert Gomez, Phil Tavlian, and Ceferino Zurita. Cef was Tommy Zurita's brother, although Cef was not a Jehovah's Witness.

Robert was kind of an intellectual bad boy. He liked to joke about sexual matters like the kind Henry Miller wrote about in *Tropic of Cancer* because he knew it would annoy a straight-laced type like me. We had an early sparring match of sorts because I was trying to write a satirical newsletter called "The Fresno Idiot" and Robert would counter with some nonsensical reply. But Robert probably became my closest high school friend.

Robert liked to mock my Arkansas heritage. I was a "dumb Arkie." I usually countered that he was a stupid Mexican. He called Phil an "Armo" because Phil was Armenian, or he made fun of Phil's unibrow. I don't remember any particular insults directed at Cef, who was the most athletic of the four of us.

Another acquaintance from those days was a guy named Ralph Whitford. Ralph and his family lived on the corner of Marks and Manning Avenue just across the street from the dairy. Ralph liked science fiction and we connected early on because of our mutual interest.

Ralph also liked to play the bad boy. He would pull the bra straps of a girl sitting in front of him in class or try to look up a girl's skirt. One time he tried to dye his hair and his hair turned pink. We parted ways more and more when I became a Jehovah's Witness.

Ralph's older brother was named Brian. Brian was the prototypical tough guy. He waited for the bus on cold foggy mornings without a jacket or even a long-sleeved shirt. He was out there in short sleeves.

At Washington Union we took our breaks and lunch at the Panther Patio. On cold days some people would light fires in the trash cans. In the background we heard KYNO radio, the dominant rock and roll radio station.

Cold and foggy mornings were part of the door to door ministry. We met early, usually at the Kingdom Hall, and someone got an assigned "territory" and we shared one or two cars to go out knocking on doors. The meetings at the Kingdom Hall featured a prayer to Jehovah and then we trooped out to separate the lambs from the goats.

When you were out door to door you always felt a little on guard. In the JW culture people are always watching you to see if you're straying from the straight and narrow. Thou shalt not criticize the Watchtower Society or show any interest in "worldly" things. You kept your hair a certain length, dressed a certain way, and limited your discussions to accepted topics.

Opie loved country music. He collected a substantial amount of music thanks to his sister-in-law Delaine. He also exchanged or collected music from a variety of other sources. It irritated Opie to hear Witnesses criticize country music. Opie attributed it to the local "brothers" and not to the people in Brooklyn. But criticism of country music was just symptomatic of the control that was a major part of the JW culture.

I could never really say it out loud, but I never liked going door to door. Religion is one of the most sensitive things you can talk about. We also tended to be out fairly early and woke people up. We tried to get around the religious sensitivity by talking about "news" in the *Awake* magazine more than the religion heavy *Watchtower*.

Some controversial Witness beliefs were also likely to come up. Not standing for the National Anthem or saluting the flag irritated some people. Some people took offense that Witnesses don't celebrate holidays like Christmas or birthdays. The refusal to accept blood transfusions, even for a child who may die without blood, was another volatile topic.

I had a dilemma one time at a school assembly over standing for the flag. The request was to stand for the parading of the colors and the National Anthem. The mention of the National Anthem made me feel that standing was inappropriate. I sat through the process despite urging from some fellow students that I would get into trouble for not standing. My teacher, who taught accounting, looked appalled, but didn't say anything to me.

I was approaching age 18 at a time when the military draft was a possibility because the Vietnam War continued to rage. My high school principal was also on my draft board. I sent the draft board a letter explaining my religious beliefs and Opie also sent a letter supporting me. I was granted conscientious objector status, but I could still have faced prison. The Watchtower Society said we could not perform alternative service.

My usual assigned seat in the school auditorium was K-9, which provided considerable amusement for some other people in my P. E. class.

Pep rallies usually happened on Friday afternoons for the football or basketball teams. I usually slipped out a little early to make it to the bus. I guess our early departure irritated the jock establishment because one afternoon several jocks were blocking the exit. It was the last pep rally I attended.

I remember Mr. Castle, my arch-conservative teacher, referred to the jock establishment as the "grunt and groaners."

Washington Union had really bad football and basketball teams during my time there. I think I went to one football game and one basketball game in my four years.

It was probably around 1968 or 1969 that my Witness friend John Shubin decided to go to Bethel at the Watchtower Headquarters in New York. People at Bethel provided volunteer labor to print the Watchtower magazines and other publications. John wound up assigned to Watchtower Farm, which provided food to the other Bethel volunteers.

In my junior year in high school I took a journalism course. It was a natural fit because I had been interested in writing since I was about ten or eleven years old. I did well enough in the journalism class to be named the news editor of *The Hatchet* in my senior year. My friend Phil Tavlian became editor-in-chief.

The Hatchet had won several awards for a high school magazine/newspaper in its class, so we wanted to maintain that standard. We went to a competition at Fresno State University. I didn't realize what I was supposed to do when a guy started talking about "open space." I wrote the best news story I could after his presentation, but my lead wasn't as strong as it should have been. I was disappointed that I didn't win an award in the news writing category.

One of the hardest things about being an editor was deciding on story assignments. The school administration had daily announcements and I used those as sources for several stories. Then there were the controversies over the way I edited stories. On one occasion a reporter was upset that I reworded a story to say "consecutive" instead of "in a row." A name was left out, but it was the reporter's omission, not my editing.

One year we had a "riot" of sorts at Washington Union. It was mostly kids milling around and not going to class. The trouble stemmed from an incident at the previous Friday night football game. I went to class, but I dutifully called the news director at KMAK Radio to report the incident.

Another bit of controversy I recall involved an advocacy group for Hispanic students called La Raza. Members of La Raza thought *The Hatchet* discriminated against Hispanic kids in its coverage. I think La Raza wanted an edition dedicated to Mexican-American students. Mr. Galdrikian, the journalism teacher, satirically wrote a list of various ethnic groups on the blackboard who might also want a special edition dedicated to their groups.

A controversy that didn't involve *The Hatchet* involved the student talent show. Some African-American kids were convinced the prize went to the wrong student. They felt the African-American participant deserved the first place award. I don't recall being impressed with anyone.

My friend Phil and I were involved in a mini-controversy over a fictional character called Augustine Sebastian. We collaborated on a short story about

Augustine Sebastian, who wore a kilt, and that caused one prudish girl some anguish. She started an anti-Augustine Sebastian petition. I wrote the staff of *Mad* magazine a letter about Augustine Sebastian and they told me they had gotten their starts working on high school newspapers.

I remember *Mad* magazine fondly. Opie had acquired a copy of *Mad* and we started going through some of the articles. I remember some satirical advertising slogans such as, "Go by Greyhound if you can't afford a bus."

Mad did a great parody of the movie *True Grit*. They called it *True Fat*. In the parody the girl Maddie never used contractions. Another great parody was of the movie *Patton* that featured a swearing and spitting Patton standing up against the Nazis.

I hated P. E class from the very beginning. I have always liked sports, but P. E. was a hierarchy of jock types against the rest of us. P. E. coaches sometimes seemed like they were drill instructors instead of teachers. Phil and I submitted an anonymous letter to *The Hatchet* blasting the P. E. coaches. Naturally, they found out who wrote the letter.

Fortunately, they didn't attempt any reprisals. One day when I was getting the towel for my shower one coach said something like, "So are you going to write something good about the coaches?" I didn't reply.

The other big P. E issue I had involved a trampoline. I don't like heights much and I wasn't comfortable bouncing around on a trampoline. I even went to see the principal to see if I could get exempted from the trampoline activity, but he wasn't very helpful.

One day we had an assembly featuring a hypnotist. He gave a post hypnotic suggestion to one student to shout, "Shut up!" and the kid actually yelled it out. I'm assuming it was legitimate.

The Hatchet had a tradition of allowing departing seniors to leave "wills." They were usually stupid things like leaving gym socks or a locker. Phil, Robert, and I left the P. E. coaches "a kick in the a__." On graduation night Robert asked me, "Should we give them what we left them?" I don't know if it was our "will" or perhaps an aggregation of rebellion that caused the school administration to discontinue senior wills.

I was reading James Michener's massive novel *Hawaii* my last week in high school. I carried the book around with me and got a few comments about the size of the book.

FIRST JOBS

Graduation from high school presented me with a dilemma. I had the academic credentials for college, but

Jehovah's Witnesses strongly discouraged college. I had no work experience and no real career expectations because, after all, the "end of the system of things" was upon us. My first "job," as it were, was cutting grapes for a farmer down the road from where we lived. The grapes were laid out on a paper "tray" to dry in the sun and transform into raisins.

Late in August and early in September migrant farm workers descend on the San Joaquin Valley to cut the grapes and when you drive out in the country you smell grapes fermenting.

Gary, John, and I cut grapes the first day and John bailed on the second day. It was hard, sweaty work. Gary and I finished the row we had been assigned.

The farmer complained at one point that we didn't have the grapes laid out well enough to get the proper exposure to the sun. We finished the row on the third day and got paid.

I used my meager proceeds to buy one of the most influential books in my life. We were at K-Mart and I was perusing the paperback books as I usually did. I saw a copy of *Ernest Hemingway: A Life Story* by Carlos Baker. I read Baker's biography, which sparked my interest in Hemingway's work, and I've been fascinated ever since.

MC DONALD'S HAMBURGERS

Then it came time to look for a job. The best solution seemed to be to use an employment agency. A company called Scope Employment Agency had frequent ads in *The Fresno Bee* and many of the jobs were in offices. My background in high school was in business, so it seemed a logical fit.

As I recall, my first interview was for an office job, but nothing came of it. I got sent for a possible job at a gas station, which was a total misfit. Mechanical objects like cars and I have a mutual antagonism. Then I got sent to McDonald's Hamburgers and got hired to fry French fries. I paid some outlandish fee to the employment agency for a truly awful job.

I got assigned to the McDonald's that was located across from the Fresno

Fairgrounds on East Kings Canyon Avenue. In those days the uniform shirt you wore zipped on the back and I was putting the thing on backwards on my first day. We also had to wear a paper hat.

Then I got introduced to frying French fries. We brought cases of frozen French fries from the freezer in the basement and carried them upstairs. Then we opened the boxes of fries and distributed them in the French fry baskets that we dropped into the hot oil. When the timer went off we took the French fries from the fryer, allowed the oil to drain, and then dumped the fries underneath a heating lamp. It wasn't a job that required much of an IQ, but it had its moments of stress, especially during heavy rushes.

After I dumped the fries, I salted them. McDonald's had a specially designed French fry scoop that fit into the bags. It took a little while to get good at using the scoop.

I met two guys I still dislike after 40 years. One guy was named Jerry Chronister. He was an assistant manager and I had to deal with him two days a week when the manager had his days off. The other guy was a mean bitter man named Derek Jones. Jones was the "grill man." He fried the hamburger patties and put the mustard and ketchup on the buns.

Chronister was a blond guy in his early twenties. He was on my back almost from the beginning. I had problems every morning lighting the gas jets for the French fry vats and it wasn't long before Chronister was griping I needed to "get faster." I used tongs to remove the fish filets from the cooking rack and Chronister complained, "I know we're not supposed to use our fingers," while he used his fingers. I suppose it was an object lesson.

Preparing the fish filets was a miserable experience because the equipment was lousy. You were supposed to steam the buns, but the steamer had a way of turning the buns into a soaking soggy mess. One time Derek Jones actually shoved me while I worked with the fish filets. I was ready to quit, but the guy at Scope Employment Agency persuaded me to stay.

Every week we got a delivery of French fries and other frozen foods and we had to stock the frozen food in the freezer downstairs. We used a ramp with rollers. One person took a package off the truck and slid it down the ramp. The person downstairs grabbed the package and hustled it into the freezer. My arm got severely bruised and the regular manager decided I shouldn't do stocking duty anymore.

I decided to change from full time to part time. Even working 15 hours a week was torturous, but it was better than being there 40 hours a week. I wanted to find another job and I discovered how difficult it was to get a job in Fresno.

It wasn't long after I started working that I bought my first car. It was a turquoise 1964 Ford Galaxie. The guy at the car dealer referred to me as a "lad." The interior had a perfume scent that made me wonder if women had used the car a great deal. It had an automatic transmission, but I had to hold the shift lever in "Park" when I started the car. Starting it first thing in the morning was quite a chore too.

Having a car allowed some freedom, but it was also restrictive. It was the first time in my life I had to deal with making payments. My Mom helped with a little bit of the car payment, but I paid the majority. There were also the costs of gas and oil and car repairs and maintenance.

When I drove the car home the first night and we got home I wasn't sure how to undo the seatbelt. I finally was able to get out, but Gary, who had ridden with me, struggled. As I've said, mechanical objects and I have a mutual antipathy.

I started running into some religious and job conflicts. Management at McDonald's liked to have occasional Saturday morning meetings, but I was supposed to be going out in the door to door ministry on Saturday mornings. When St. Patrick's Day came McDonald's featured a mint green milkshake and they wanted us to wear hats honoring St. Patrick's Day. I told the manager that St. Patrick's Day had religious significance and I couldn't wear the hat. I overhead someone asking why the "fry guy" (me) wasn't wearing the hat.

I remember how happy I was on Friday evenings when I knew I didn't have to go fry French fries the next day. There were shows like "The Odd Couple" and "Love American Style" on television and I associate them with free Saturdays.

I got a break when Jerry Chronister moved to a different McDonald's, which they called a "store."

In 1972 Frank Toste moved his dairy operations from Marks and Manning to near Kerman, California. He built several new houses for his employees and we moved into a new house on Bishop Avenue.

The new location meant a longer commute to Fresno. Gas was relatively cheap back then, but it seemed expensive on my limited income of $1.65 an hour. Having to drive farther was also a problem in the fog season.

The move also meant that Gary and John were in the Kerman School District. Gary decided he wanted to continue at Washington Union and got a transfer agreement.

I started attending meetings at the Kerman Kingdom Hall of Jehovah's Witnesses. It was a fresh start. I was disillusioned with the Fresno South Congregation in Easton and I thought it might make a difference in a new congregation.

I met Sam Roberson, the "congregation servant," and James Childrey, and Paul Long. Roberson was a big and rather charismatic man who was destined for bigger things in the organization of Jehovah's Witnesses. James Childrey was an African-American man married to a white woman. I remember him constantly saying, "Really good, really fine." Paul Long was a sign painter who had moved to Kerman from Santa Cruz.

Another guy I met was John Daniels. John was a quiet and humble guy who didn't talk much. He was a skilled mechanic and ran his own janitorial business. He drove a car that had previously been a police cruiser.

Paul Long interested me because of his sign painting business. I liked creative things and sign painting was the most creative occupation I found among Jehovah's Witnesses I had met. Paul lived in a little house in Kerman that was overrun with cockroaches and he had a black Labrador dog. Paul had reportedly had drug problems before joining "the truth."

Paul said he learned sign painting from a "brother." He didn't have a car and he was constantly trying to find rides to do his sign painting work. He liked Merle Haggard and he borrowed Gary's album where Hag did a tribute to Jimmie Rogers.

In 1971 and 1972 I lost my grandfather and my Aunt Hattie and Uncle Thurman. My grandfather died in a Hanford, California, rest home. My aunt and uncle were killed by a drunk driver in an automobile accident.

Gary graduated early at Washington Union and moved back to Arkansas to live with our father and his wife Fran. My father had made some promises about getting Gary a good job. The "good job" turned out to be working in a chicken plant.

Fran wasn't happy about Gary being there and he started spending time with my stepfather's relatives. My Mom wasn't happy about that and she suggested I write Gary a letter.

He sent me back a rather hateful letter about how I needed to "get my own head together." I never felt about him quite the same after that.

While he was there Gary also regaled people with accounts of using drugs. I always thought it was nonsense. Gary didn't even have money to buy drugs. But he seemed to have a need for attention and the drug story was a good way to get attention.

SAM ROBERSON AND PAUL LONG

After I had been at McDonald's a year, Sam Roberson offered me a job doing janitorial work. Sam had run a janitorial business for a while and he was reportedly called "Spotless Sam."

I went with him on a few janitorial jobs and then he gave me the key to an office that he cleaned. I was going to try cleaning it on my own. I went to the office and completed the work and went home. Then I got a call from him that I needed to come back to the office. We went inside and he found things he didn't like. He decided to steer me toward working with Paul Long in the sign painting business.

Sam considered himself an astute businessman. He wanted to try selling things at a local auction called the Cherry Auction. I had been to the Cherry Auction to look around and even to do a modified version of the door-to-door ministry. We took copies of *The Watchtower* and *Awake* magazines and tried to place them. I remember I also bought a paperback copy of a book by Moss Hart called *Act One* from someone selling books.

One night I was riding with Sam and he started talking about demons and how maybe demons subsisted on some kind of "energy food." Another time he was driving and reading from a talk he had prepared. People driving and reading at the same time has always made me nervous.

I was at a meeting one Sunday morning and sitting next to Paul Long. Sam was on the platform and said, "I heard a song this morning that said 'I've got the hungries for your love.'" Paul Long leaned over and said, "Buck Owens." It was a song called "Waitin' In Your Welfare Line." It was a song Opie hated because it perpetuated the stereotype that everyone getting public assistance was a freeloader.

I had a relatively low lottery number in the military draft and I got a notice for a pre-induction physical. Vietnam was still going strong in 1972. President Nixon had initiated a lottery system to make the draft more politically acceptable. I had already been classified a conscientious objector because of my Jehovah's Witness beliefs, but I still faced possible prison because I couldn't perform alternative service.

There was no way it could be a positive experience. You were in a group of other young men and forced to undergo things like the infamous hernia test and a check for hemorrhoids. You had your hearing tested and vision tested and blood taken. You took a written test. You were asked if you were homosexual. I vehemently said I wasn't homosexual and the interviewer said, "You must *want* to get drafted." I said that no, I was classified a CO. I had some luck because the government stopped calling numbers before they reached my number in the lottery.

After Sam Roberson decided I wasn't meant for janitorial work, he suggested I partner with Paul Long in Long's sign painting business. Paul Long didn't have a car and needed transportation. Initially, I thought it was going to be a partnership, but I eventually found out Long had different ideas.

We talked about a name for the business. I suggested Arrowhead Signs, but Sam Roberson thought that name sounded too much like a boys' club. We settled on the name "Long's Signs."

My friend Tommy Zurita had taken over a printing business in Easton previously owned by congregation overseer William Burdine. Burdine and his family moved to Kentucky, where the Watchtower Society said "the need was great" as Armageddon approached. He then sold his printing business to Tommy.

Paul Long and I met with Tommy to arrange to print business cards for the newly-coined Long's Signs.

The first sign painting job I remember was a Monroe Shock Absorbers sign in Madera. It was a large sign on top of a building. The sign had to be scaled and Paul hired a larger sign company in Fresno to do the scaling. He got what was in essence a stencil that outlined the letters of the sign.

The "stencil" was a long piece of brown paper. He took what was called a "pounce wheel" to perforate the letters of the sign. He then aligned the "stencil" on the wall and attached it. He took a bag of colored chalk and tapped the bag against the "stencil" to outline each letter against the wall.

Paul did the skilled work on the edge of the letters and I did the easier fill in work. I had to climb a ladder to get to the sign and that bothered me because I've never liked heights. Once I got up to the top it wasn't too bad because there was a wide deck to stand on.

Paul painted various kinds of signs. He did lettering for trucks and for windows and for signs that attached to walls. I remember a cold night when he was doing the lettering on a truck door. I waited inside the house and read a little of *The Grapes of Wrath* by John Steinbeck.

On a sign painting trip to Madera I found a used copy of Hemingway short stories in a store. I got introduced to "Big Two-Hearted River," my all-time favorite short story and "The Battler," another of my favorites.

I got a library card at the Madera Library. I tried to read when I was waiting for Paul Long on his sign painting jobs.

Our agreement was that I got a commission for sign work I found for Paul and I got paid per mile for transporting him. But it became apparent to me pretty quickly that there would not be enough volume for me to make any real money.

Paul started courting a Mexican-American woman named Isabel and Isabel quickly had an influence on Paul after they got married. He started acting like a boss and not a partner. He complained that we were getting started too late and he wanted me at his place earlier in the morning. I wasn't too happy about being ordered like an employee and I didn't comply. Our relationship began to deteriorate.

He had a job in Madera that required a scaffold so he could work on the sign. Someone yelled from a car on the street, "You're gonna fall! You're gonna fall!"

We carried paint cans in the trunk of my car. One of the cans spilled over and we left white tire tracks in the Kingdom Hall parking lot.

Around Christmas Paul went with Isabel to his home town Santa Cruz. He suggested I could solicit business while he was out of town. But by then I wasn't enthused and I took the time off. That didn't make him happy either.

Another time Paul strapped a sign to the top of my car. As we drove a gust of wind caught the sign and buckled it. Paul ordered me to pull next to a vacant building. He took the sign off the car and went into the building with a hammer and began furiously hammering the buckled area on the sign and trying to repair the damage to the paint. He fired the hammer against the wall. I was glad I wasn't standing in the way.

One or two lectures too many finally persuaded me to look for a more conventional job and I left the sign painting business.

MISCELLANEOUS JOBS IN 1973

The next job I found was making telephone calls for a company called Handicapped Workers. Handicapped workers supposedly made things like light bulbs and I called people to sell them the light bulbs or other products. I'm not very aggressive and after a few days I wasn't selling enough to suit the management. After I left, the company skipped town and it took some government intervention to get the last remaining pay I was due.

I remember one of the other callers was into chess. He liked looking at chess problems in the newspaper and trying to solve them.

The next job was also calling people. It was for a company called Pine Mountain Lake. They sold vacation homes up in the mountains. My job was to call prospective buyers and set up appointments for the salesmen. People who responded also got a "free gift."

The job was part-time and in the evening. I worked with a guy named Dave Holderman, who just a little younger than me. Dave had a great voice and aspired to be a radio announcer.

The office manager was a guy named Herb and I remember he had a really attractive secretary, but I don't recall her name. I got frustrated after a while and one night Herb listened in on a call and then advised me to call back and I persuaded the person to schedule an appointment.

One night some of Dave Holderman's friends came by and we got into a discussion about gay people. At the time I was virulently anti-gay because of my Jehovah's Witness beliefs. I remember saying things like gay people should be shot. I like to think I've come a long way since then.

After a few months, the upper management decided to discontinue the phone operation.

I tried a sales job selling Rexair Rainbow vacuum cleaners. The distinctive feature about Rexair Rainbows was its water filtration system.

I went to a recruitment meeting one afternoon and took a test. I don't know if the test was legitimate or if everyone "passed" the test. Then I went through the training to learn to sell the Rexair Rainbow.

Our presentation emphasized how poorly conventional vacuum cleaners did the job as opposed to the great job done by the Rexair Rainbow. We would turn on a conventional vacuum cleaner and hold up a lamp to show the dust particles floating in the air because the dust slipped through the dry filter system. Then we would clean an area with the Rexair and the water would turn brown and muddy.

At the end of the presentation we asked people to complete a small questionnaire. Their answers indicated if they would probably buy the Rexair. We made a pretense of calling the office with the results of the questionnaire.

We also asked people to give us names of friends or relatives who might be interested in a free presentation of the Rexair. That was the way leads were generated.

What attracted me to the job in the first place was the claim you could make $500 a month. It was misleading at best. The only way you could make a guaranteed $500 was to do an incredible number of presentations. Otherwise, you had to make the money from sales.

I did a presentation for my friend Tommy and sold a vacuum cleaner to him. I sold just enough to move up in the ranks of dealers.

When you moved up the dealer ladder you could train other dealers and get a percentage of any sales they made. I remember spending the day with a guy who got frustrated by his treatment by management and he quit.

I did a presentation for a fellow Jehovah's Witness in Kerman. He sold Kirby vacuum cleaners. His wife liked the Rexair and he didn't and that amused my boss at Rexair.

One time I spent a long day trying to sell, including a trip to Reedley. In my conversation with the guy I mentioned Huey Long. I had read the T. Harry Williams biography of Long a little earlier. The guy said something to the effect that you read about Huey Long, but I lived through that time.

On the way home I smelled the sweet scent of flowers blooming and I still think of that night when I smell something similar.

The owner of the local franchise really pushed sales one day, but the results didn't satisfy him. The next day his office staff didn't even attempt to make any appointments for the sales staff. That was my cue to leave the vacuum cleaner business.

I got a job at the Denny's near Jensen and Freeway 99 in Fresno. I was a dishwasher and bus boy. The dishwashing job was hard, but much easier than being a bus boy. A former classmate at Washington Union was cooking for Denny's. The main dishwasher was a Jehovah's Witness.

Waitresses and bus boys were always on the move and it was easy to crash into someone. One waitress would always warn me, "Behind you."

One of my duties was vacuuming the carpet. One afternoon I was vacuuming an area with no people, but a guy sitting in a different area complained and I had to stop.

I wasn't enamored of the job at Denny's and my friend Tommy Zurita mentioned an opening at Frank J. Sanders Body Shop. A guy named David Gonzalez, who was also a Jehovah's Witness, worked at the body shop. My job was to be a go-fer and cleanup guy.

I went to the body shop one morning and expected to be interviewed, but I was immediately hired. The whole job was a disaster. There was a supervisor named Mac who was always on my back. My fellow Jehovah's Witness was never any help at all (a pattern I saw frequently).

I had to check the cars on the lot in the afternoon to make sure the keys were removed. I must have missed one and the car got stolen. I also had to drive a pickup on errands and I had an accident with the pickup that resulted in scraped paint on the right side. It was disappointing to get fired, but a relief of sorts too.

I moved on to a job with R. L. Polk gathering information for the city directory. You got assigned a territory that you covered going door to door. I had a printed list of addresses and names and I tried to verify if the same people lived at the address that appeared on the list. Someone told me there were some fake names on the list to catch people who didn't actually verify the names.

I've never been a big fan of public contact and the job was too much like going door to door as a Jehovah's Witness. Some people were also incredibly suspicious. I remember one person said, "I *know* who you are."

One of the houses I checked belonged to the former mayor of Fresno, Ted C. Wills.

I ran into older people who were probably lonely and who wanted to talk. That caused me some problems with a sourpuss of a supervisor at R. L. Polk, who thought my production was too low. That was despite the fact I actually cheated myself out of some time because I made some allowances for the long conversations.

One thing I remember from that period is a Dolly Parton song called "Jolene." It got played a good deal on the radio and the chorus of "Jolene, Jolene, Jolene" still grates on my nerves.

1974

I naively thought I could try to be a free-lance writer for the next few months. I sent out manuscripts coupled with my hopes and dreams and with the thought I could surely sell something and make as much as I had made at the terrible jobs I'd worked at until then. Then reality came along with the rejection slips.

I contacted the Scope Employment Agency again. They were the same employment agency I had worked with years before to get the job at McDonald's. Initially, it seemed this experience would be better. I got sent on an interview for a copywriting job with an advertising agency. But nothing came of it and the next interview was with a local convenience store chain called Zip 'N Go.

I had to take a lie detector test as part of the hiring process. I got hired. The store sold gas and the usual convenience store items.

I spent just a few days at Zip 'N Go. On the first day there I worked by myself because the other person scheduled to work didn't come to work. I was overwhelmed. I didn't know where the key was to the ice machine outside. Someone sent a kid to buy cigarettes and I declined because the kid was too young. Someone else claimed I hadn't given back the correct change.

I expected Scope Agency to contact me, but they didn't contact me for several days. By then I knew I didn't want to stay at Zip 'N Go and I didn't want to pay another outrageous fee to Scope Agency. As far as I was concerned, they didn't get me the kind of job I was seeking in media or journalism.

When I talked to the job recruiter at Scope he said they had worked long and hard for me. I wrote them a letter and sent them most of the meager salary I had made at Zip 'N Go. I told them I wasn't going to give them everything I had made.

I told them they had sent me to McDonald's, which was a job I hated, and I had paid them an exorbitant fee for that. Then they didn't get me the kind of job I was seeking. They sent me back an indignant and rather self-righteous letter about how I was taking advantage of *them*. I'm happy that Scope Agency and similar type employment agencies don't exist much anymore.

Then I wound up working two nights a week at a 7-11 store. I worked the graveyard shift on Friday and Saturday nights. The job mostly involved cleaning the store, mopping the floor, organizing the shelves, and restocking stuff in the freezer.   There was also the occasional customer.

I found out that you couldn't sell beer from about 2 a. m. until 6 a. m. I don't know the reason for that law, but it was one of those things that could create conflict. I learned that when you organized the shelves you moved items up to the front to make the shelves look full. It was called "facing." I learned that wearing a jacket was a good idea when I worked in the freezer, but some people thought it was weird to be wearing a jacket in warm weather.

The guy who owned the 7-11 was named Bert Contreras. Bert, to put it kindly, was thrifty. His idea of security was a baseball bat. He used the video surveillance tape until it wore out. He *did* have a phone that went directly to his home phone.

One night some teenagers came in after 2 a. m. and grabbed some beer and ran out of the store. I rang Bert's number and he recognized them from the description I gave.

Another night I kept getting ridiculous phone calls asking what kind of fast food was available. Then they would hang up and call again in a few minutes. An African-American customer took the phone from me and said, "What's the matter with you?"

A guy came in one morning and asked for a pack of cigarettes. I put the cigarettes on the counter and he just walked out without paying. I guess I could have brandished the baseball bat, but somehow it didn't seem worth it.

A customer who got on my nerves was a guy who came in to skim the magazines. He would stand there skimming the magazines and I couldn't do anything else until he left.

Some young kids came in one night and wanted to help me. I don't know why they were out, but I let them do simple things like carry out the trash.

We were supposed to ask for ID for anyone buying liquor if they looked younger than 21. I know I blew it with one kid. He gave me the old line about not having his ID with him, but I'm convinced he was younger than 21.

I remember a guy coming in one morning and getting some coffee. He was getting ready to go on a fishing trip. He told me, "You're a nice guy, but you make lousy coffee."

I've never smoked or been around people who smoked, so I didn't really know the protocol. I sold some cigarettes to a guy one night and he asked for matches. I gave him a pack of matches, which I guess wasn't enough, and he was upset. Another customer asked for Zig Zags, a kind of cigarette paper. I had no idea at the time what Zig Zags were.

One time a customer complained about the pepperoni sticks. It didn't occur to him I had nothing to do with the buying and stocking of the merchandise.

After a few months at 7-11 I was restive and I wanted to move on. I thought maybe I could get some kind of writing job somewhere else. So I was considering a move to Portland, Oregon.

I packed a few things, including some books, and drove to Modesto to see my aunt Ruby and Opie. Opie suggested Sacramento might be an alternative to going all the way to Portland. So I went to Sacramento and stayed a night. I realized quickly that I didn't have enough money to survive for very long and I didn't know what to do. I wound up going back to Modesto.

As I think back, I regret that I spent time with my aunt and cousin because I know it had to put a financial strain on them. They were poor and already had limited resources and they certainly didn't need me depleting their resources even more. But it wasn't because I wasn't trying to do something positive.

Opie advised me to apply for unemployment. Initially, I got turned down because I had quit the job at 7-11. But they said if I made a certain amount of money I could qualify for unemployment. I got a job at Mervyn's Department Store for the Christmas season and I was almost obsessed with how close I was to making the necessary money to qualify for unemployment.

The job was typical of temporary jobs I've had. You get thrown into the fray with little training. So you tend to run around trying to get someone to answer your questions and not getting much help.

One morning I was in the store early when some other employees showed up outside and needed to be let into the store. I didn't know how to open the door, so I had to go find help. I felt a little like Lassie.

I had one dress shirt I wore to work every day, but Mervyn's was the first job I didn't dread every day. I worked through the Christmas season and made enough money to qualify for unemployment.

I spent lots of time with Opie, of course. His room had a kind of brown wood paneling on the walls. I always associate the scent of shaving lotion with

Opie. He had a pretty good collection of aftershaves. He had a fondness for pullover shirts because they were easier to put on and take off than the buttoning version. He had terrible headaches, so he took massive amounts of aspirin.

For as long as I knew him Opie loved soft drinks. Pepsi was his beverage of choice, but he drank Tab for a while. I never liked Tab all that much, but I developed a taste for Pepsi.

Opie became quite the music collector. He would record almost anything if he got offered the opportunity. His friend Roy Shaw brought an album by a singer named Maria Muldaur. She had a song called "Midnight at the Oasis." Opie liked the song and when he liked a song he tended to play it over and over.

Another song I remember him playing was John Denver's "Back Home Again."

The author I remember reading the most then was Herman Wouk. I read *Marjorie Morningstar* and it seems like I read *The Caine Mutiny* and *Youngblood Hawke*.

Opie didn't like television much. He liked game shows like "Jeopardy" and "Hollywood Squares." He liked "The Tonight Show" and "60 Minutes." Sometimes if a psychic appeared on "The Tonight Show" he turned off the TV because of fear of "demonism."

But I do remember watching some of the entertainment shows from that time. There was "Chico and the Man" with Freddie Prinze, "The Rockford Files" with James Garner, "Sanford and Son," and "Movin' On" with the theme song sung by Merle Haggard. Opie and I watched baseball and football too.

After I started to get unemployment Opie obviously wanted me to get an apartment. He was concerned he would get into trouble with the welfare authorities because I wasn't supposed to be there. I found a small place on Lita Court in Modesto. It was really more like a small house than a typical apartment. It had a bath, a kitchen, and a living room/bedroom combination.

He loaned me money to get a second hand television and I did my grocery shopping at a place called Prairie Market.

Prairie Market was a discount grocery store. One of the interesting quirks they had was that you marked prices on the merchandise yourself rather than having the prices already there. The prices were posted on the shelves where the products were located and you used a marker to mark the prices on the merchandise.

I didn't have a phone at the apartment, so I had to use Opie's number. The Employment Development Dept. people called one day about a temporary job. It involved carrying a sample of a new soap product door to door and leaving the sample for the homeowner. You had to yell out "Free sample" as you approached the door. They wanted the bottle placed so that one side faced the street.

They drove us around in a van and then we got out to walk and carried a box of laundry detergent like an army field pack. After a while my feet started to blister and I told the supervisor I couldn't walk anymore. You always worry in a situation like that if the Dept. of Employment Development will cut off your unemployment benefits.

I did have to endure an EDD "interview," but I continued my unemployment benefits.

As spring approached and baseball spring training started, we learned that the San Francisco Giants and California Angels were scheduled to play an exhibition game in Modesto. Opie and I had been out to the ballpark to watch the Modesto A's play, but a major league game would be really special. The game was going to be even more special because pitching legend Nolan Ryan was scheduled to start for the Angels.

I stayed for several hours at the sporting goods store that was selling tickets to buy tickets to the game. When game day arrived it was overcast and drizzly, but there wasn't any serious rain. We got to the ballpark and even talked to a member of the Angels. But then Dick Williams, who was managing the Angels, decided the game should be called because of rain.

The next day a columnist for *The Modesto Bee* criticized the decision to call the game. Opie and I wrote a letter to the Baseball Commissioner's Office to complain, but all we got was a formulaic response that they would review the umpires' reports and there was never any formal apology.

WORKING FOR OPIE

As spring came on, my aunt Ruby's health deteriorated. She had been in poor health for some time. She couldn't lie down at night, so she slept sitting up in a chair. He legs were swollen and red. She was hospitalized.

My aunt Erma Jean was in town and my Mom was also in town. I was sleeping in Opie's room when the phone rang. Opie asked me to pick up the extension. I heard my cousin Bob tell my aunt Erma Jean that Ruby had died. I didn't immediately tell Opie. I told him we needed to get up. I pushed his wheelchair into the living room and my aunt Erma Jean told him, "Your mama died last night."

Opie decided not to attend the funeral. Some people thought it was because he was a Jehovah's Witness, but he told me it was because he "just couldn't take it." Prior to her death, Opie had told me he was concerned about her weight and eating habits. He also said she was a good Mom.

Stanislaus County had a program that allowed a handicapped person like Opie to hire a home health care worker to help take care of them and Opie suggested I could try that. We apportioned our expenses based on income and I paid more because I had a better income than he did.

My cousin Bob owned the house where Opie and my aunt lived. He suggested we could do some repainting to help deal with grieving over her loss. I got green paint for her former room and Opie selected a kind of orange paint for portions of his room. Opie also wanted to paint the front sidewalk. He said his mother had always resisted painting the sidewalk and it was something he wanted to do.

We bought a chemical to prepare the concrete for painting and then we painted the sidewalk red.

I learned to cook basic things. We also had a barbecue to thank Opie's brothers for their help. Bob and Thurman did the barbecuing.

My former landlord on Lita Court refused to give me back my security deposit, claiming I hadn't left the apartment as clean as I'd found it. A tile had come up on the floor and a mattress cover had torn. I didn't consider either of those things my fault. I finally gave up, although I wrote a couple of places, such as the fire department, about the landlord.

I had always loved visits to Modesto and seeing Opie and Ruby. But I found out day to day living with Opie wasn't quite the same. Life was boring for one thing. He didn't like TV and we really couldn't go many places. About the only books Opie kept were Watchtower Society publications.

Opie had a kind of sardonic wit that could be cutting. Gary had a weight problem for as long as I can remember, for instance, and Opie made insulting remarks about Gary's weight. I didn't know until years later how much the "jokes" had hurt Gary.

Some of his jokes were predictable: If you heard the wind blowing, Opie would say, "What do you call that?" The answer was "Mariah."

Our lives settled into routine. We went to meetings at the Kingdom Hall on

Thursday and on Sunday unless Opie had one of his excruciating headaches. We went to the Tuesday night book study at a private home within walking distance of the house.

We talked about taking a road trip and visiting my old Witness friends John Shubin and Paul Long. John Shubin was living over in the Watsonville area and Paul Long was still in Kerman. I called them both and got very cool responses, so we decided to call off the trip. Paul Long told me that Sam Roberson had become a circuit overseer and he gave me his address. I wrote Sam Roberson, but never got a response.

We had some bizarre arguments. One time I had a debate with Opie about the so-called "silent e" that you find in a lot of English words. For example, the word "home" has a silent "e" on the end. Opie insisted he could hear the silent "e."

Another time someone brought a book called *The Memory Book*. It was written by a former basketball star named Jerry Lucas. The book dealt with tricks and techniques to memorize almost anything.

Opie wanted to try it and he wanted a list of words to memorize. I made a list and he got mad because he wasn't familiar with some of the words.

On another occasion we were having problems with a swamp cooler that was leaking. I went to find Opie and discovered him in his electric wheelchair armed with a hoe. He was ready to beat the swamp cooler into submission.

As I was becoming more disaffected from Jehovah's Witnesses, Opie wanted to immerse himself even more. He made contact with some Witnesses in the country of Guyana and wanted to send them small cassette recorders. I admired his generosity, but I wondered if people were taking advantage of him sometimes.

He talked about moving to a house next door to the Kingdom Hall, which didn't appeal to me. He had some Witnesses over as guests one afternoon and one of the men wanted Opie to record all the "Kingdom music" onto cassettes for him. The Watchtower

Society had released a record set that featured the music used in meetings. It was a massive project and took a lot of Opie's time.

One thing we continued to share was loving baseball. Opie was an Oakland A's fan. The A's won the World Series three straight years: 1972, 1973, and 1974. They were in the American League Championship Series in 1975 against the Boston Red Sox, but lost.

The Red Sox were matched up against the Cincinnati Reds in the World Series. This was a Cincinnati team that featured players like Johnny Bench, Pete Rose, and Dave Concepcion. The Series went back and forth, but Cincinnati took a three games to two lead and they were leading in Game 6. They were mere outs away from winning the Series.

It appeared the Reds were in control. The Red Sox had the tying run at the plate and Bernie Carbo was the hitter. Carbo looked struck out on one pitch, but managed to foul off the pitch. Then Carbo launched a homerun that tied the game and the real drama began.

Red Sox right fielder Dwight Evans made a spectacular game-saving catch. The game went into extra innings and then Carlton Fisk hit the homerun that is immortalized in film. It shows him trotting down the first base line and urging the ball to stay fair.

The Reds won game seven and the World Series the following day.

I felt more and more trapped. I was essentially committed 24/7 to staying with Opie. I remember being really disappointed one day when he changed his mind about going out to a store because I had been looking forward to getting out of the house.

I'm not sure if things with Opie deteriorated immediately, or because he got mad one morning because I had kept my bedroom door closed. I ordinarily kept the door open so I could hear him, but for some reason that night I closed the door.

I found him trying to get out of bed and over the next few days he made noises about becoming more independent. He talked about possibly doing some kind of job for his brother Bob, for instance. I finally decided it was time for me to return to Fresno.

Fortunately, I was eligible for unemployment. I moved back to Fresno in February, 1976, and stayed at my Mom and stepfather's house on the dairy near Kerman, drew unemployment, and looked for a job.

I was angry with Opie and I sent him a letter that started, "Dear Edwards." I wanted to find out about getting the books I had left behind at his house. He sent me back a rather cold letter that started, "Dear Goodwin."

We had intermittent contacts over the next few years. I saw him when he came to Fresno for a district assembly of Jehovah's Witnesses. I had moved to an apartment complex near Fresno State University and I remember the weather was hot because it was June or July. I saw him in the motel room where he was staying with some other Witnesses.

He had an attaché case with cassettes arranged in alphabetical order. They contained country music recordings.

The last time I saw him was in October, 1982, during the World Series. The Milwaukee Brewers were playing the

St. Louis Cardinals. One of the Witnesses Opie knew came over to his apartment and demonstrated pretty quickly he didn't know anything about baseball.

I remember taking some new albums for him to record, including an album by country music star John Anderson. He treated me to dinner at a Mexican restaurant. It was amusing when mariachi singers came around to our table. I played very bad chess against a Witness friend of his. I saw a note from the woman he would eventually marry and then lose to cancer.

I remember the way he looked when I was leaving to go back home. He frequently sat off to the side of his wheelchair and that was how he sat as I drove away.

We didn't have much contact after that. I heard through the proverbial grapevine that he was getting married. I sent him a brief note asking if that was true. After that, we didn't have contact. I found out subsequently that the Watchtower Society considered those of us not active in the organization to be the equivalent of disfellowshipped people, which meant that good Witnesses would have no contact with us.

I got word from my cousin Linda in January, 2001, that Opie had died. He went to the doctor for a procedure. They left him alone and he aspirated. It was undoubtedly a case of medical negligence. By that time Opie had remarried and even adopted a child. His second wife slipped away with the child and left their mobile home and other possessions behind.

GUARANTEE SAVINGS AND LOAN

I became a fan of the mini-series "Rich Man, Poor Man" broadcast in 1976. It was based on an Irwin Shaw novel and it was a major starring vehicle for Nick Nolte. I started my job hunt and applied for a vault teller job through an employment agency.

I got sent instead for an interview for a loan teller position at Guarantee Savings and Loan. Guarantee was a venerable institution in Fresno. It was started in Fresno in 1919 and had branches throughout the San Joaquin

Valley. The symbol associated with Guarantee was a Motel T truck with the word "Guarantee" written across the door.

I got hired for a loan teller position in April, 1976. I went to the office complex at 1318 E. Shaw in Fresno. Guarantee had built two four-story buildings referred to as the East Tower and the West Tower. I think zoning regulations prevented building one eight-story building.

The loan teller position involved preparing loan documents for signature. My first job was working at an automatic typewriter called an IBM 3735. You loaded the information needed to start typing documents and then you adjusted the documents as the typewriter filled in the blanks. It wasn't the most exciting job, but it was far better than other jobs I had worked at until then.

My supervisor was a perky woman named Pat Thompson. Pat was one of those people who exuded perkiness. I got along well with Pat for the most part, although we had some friction later on.

After I worked on the 3735 for a while, I learned to enter information on a computer terminal called a CRT. We filled in the information about the loan on the CRT and that information was then transferred to the loan documents when they were printed on the 3735.

I didn't really know how to dress for an office and I didn't have the funds to buy clothes even if I had known how to dress. I typically wore something like a leisure suit jacket, a shirt and clip-on tie, and cowboy boots. I had become a big fan of cowboy boots while I lived in Modesto.

Things went reasonably well and I got offered a chance to move to the Loan Disbursement area. I spent my time in that department for several years.

A lady named Shirley Motley worked with construction loans paying construction vouchers to contractors and subcontractors. Tricia Hogue had trained me on the 3735 and she was working on finalizing loans that had closed escrow.

Janet Headrick was the best supervisor I ever had.

I've always been shy and it was never easy acclimating myself to a new situation, but it wasn't long before I developed a good working relationship with everyone in the Disbursement Dept.

My job involved cutting checks to title and escrow companies on new loans, putting the finishing touches on loans that had closed escrow, and paying some construction vouchers.

Janet knew that dealing with customers was difficult for me, so she tried to minimize my having to pay vouchers over the counter. It wasn't too bad as long as you could actually pay the voucher, but it was harder when you ran into a problem.

A typical construction loan was set up with a voucher system. There were some loans that involved one large payment to the contractor each time a stage of construction (called progress pay) was completed, but they were relatively rare. Vouchers were similar to checks. As work was completed by subcontractors, the primary contractor wrote a voucher for the work that was completed such as framing, drywall, etc.

The subcontractor then mailed the voucher to us or brought it in person. We checked the category the subcontractor was being paid for, such as framing, made sure there was still money available for that item, and that the appraisal department had done an inspection to verify the work was actually completed.

If the item was overdrawn by more than a certain percentage, we had to get the voucher approved by the appraisal department. We ran into particular problems with vouchers for appliances because appliances could be easily removed from the new home and the money would no longer be available to pay for new appliances.

When Tricia got married and left the company I moved into her position and a guy named Steve Civiello became the new funding clerk.

Steve struck me as a guy who worked very hard to strike a persona. He was freshly out of the military and part of his approach was to look tough. He also seemed determined, no matter what, that we were going to be bosom buddies. The problem was that we didn't have much in common and I didn't really like him very much.

It wasn't that I didn't make at least some effort to like him. When he first came to Guarantee, for instance, I went to lunch with him at a restaurant called The Big Yellow House that was within walking distance of the Guarantee Towers. He said he had smoked a form of marijuana called Thai Sticks while he was in the Navy and stationed in Thailand. I heard about calamari, fried squid, but I don't remember much else of substance.

When we got word that Steve would move to Disbursements I wasn't enthused. It was like working around a ticking time bomb. I remember one time he had a dispute with Janet and Shirley and he told me, "I would kill for you, but I wouldn't for them."

An older lady who worked for Guarantee then was Sandy Wolfe. Sandy was in charge of writing loan procedures and preparing memos for Ken Forsyth, our department manager. She was probably one of the most territorial people I ever encountered.

Some people may have considered Sandy an accomplished writer, but it seemed to me that most of the procedures she wrote came almost directly from bulletins issued by the Savings and Loan Institute.

As things began to change in the savings and loan business, it seemed Sandy had a hard time making adjustments. For example, variable loans came into existence in the 1980's. Prior to that, most loans were written for a fixed interest rate over the entire term of the loan. But banks and other lenders didn't like fixed interest rates because of the impact of inflation. Adjustable or variable loans helped to negate the effects of inflation for lenders.

Sandy wrote the procedures for variable loans, but she never seemed to really understand them. At Guarantee we called them Adjustable Mortgage Loans (AML's). Jack Good was the name of the guy who conceived the various loans Guarantee offered.

One thing that irritated me was the use of Roman numerals in naming the loans. It was an AML V, instead of AML 5, for instance. I remember telling Pam Edwards, who was my boss then, that it made more sense to use regular Arabic numbers instead of Roman numerals. Using Roman numerals led to too many mistakes.

After I had been at Guarantee a few months, I moved into Fresno to an apartment complex near the Veteran's Hospital on Clinton and Fresno Street. Gary was already living in an apartment there.

It was essentially a studio apartment. The living room and bedroom merged together and there was a kitchen and bathroom. The floor was linoleum and I don't recall any carpeting at all. I didn't even have a phone for a very long time. The strongest memory I have of the place is that it always smelled like gas.

In 1977 I was driving home in the Pinto I drove then. It wasn't running well and I tried to make an ill-advised left turn and got clobbered. The rear passenger side fender was badly damaged, but the car was still drivable. The process of getting the car fixed was a lesson in how difficult it was to get help if you didn't have any money.

My Mom and stepfather were kind enough to let me drive one of their cars while I tried to get the Pinto repaired. I tried to get a loan from one of Guarantee's subsidiaries with no success, but somehow I managed to get the Pinto fixed.

Another incident, far more minor, with the Pinto occurred when I was buying self-service gas at a Gemco station. I was behind a car and a lady pulled up fairly close behind me. When I was trying to edge the Pinto out I barely touched the bumper of the car in front. The lady claimed there was a scratch on the bumper. I referred her and her husband to my insurance company. I was told the woman and her husband even came to my workplace, but I wasn't there at the time.

I first joined a book club while I was living at the 20th Century Apartments. One book I remember from that period was a short story collection by Irwin Shaw.

Other things I associate with that apartment complex are the premier of the original "Battlestar Galactica" show, which was a disappointment to me, the Oakland Raiders winning their first Super Bowl, the famous (or infamous) "fumblerooski" incident that gave the Raiders a win over the San Diego Chargers in 1978, and taking a creative writing class at Fresno City College.

Things at Guarantee were going reasonably well. An opening occurred in Sandy Wolfe's department and Ken Forsyth wanted me to move to that position. It involved writing procedures and memos. But it didn't take long for me to realize I didn't want to be there and that I preferred being in Disbursements.

Ken Forsyth wasn't happy when I approached him about returning to my prior job. I told him I liked to leave work at work and he made some comment about how the world wouldn't have progressed if everyone had an attitude like that. I had to endure some drama over a few days, but finally got to return to Disbursements.

In 1979 I decided it was time to move. I rented a second story apartment a few blocks from the Guarantee Towers. It was close to Fresno State University and the new football stadium. I liked the location because it allowed me to walk to and from work.

When I first started at Guarantee the area behind the Towers was a huge parking lot. They decided to build additional one story office buildings in that area. One of the new businesses was a store from the locally-based Custer's Last Sandwich Stand.

I liked the avocado and cream cheese sandwich they sold at Custer's. It came with alfalfa sprouts. I've never found a comparable sandwich since then.

When I was at Guarantee I customarily took my vacation in October. The Orioles were in the postseason a good deal back then and I wanted a chance to see the games if they actually made it to the playoffs. In 1979 they were in the World Series against the Pittsburgh Pirates.

The Orioles looked as though they were going to win another World Series. They took a three games to one lead with the last two games to be played in Baltimore. Jim Palmer and Scott McGregor were scheduled to start games six and seven and I couldn't think of two better pitchers to close out a World Series.

I remember getting off work and stopping by Custer's for the avocado and cream cheese sandwich and going home to watch the World Series.

The O's couldn't close the deal and Pittsburgh won the Series in seven games.

After I moved I continued to grocery shop at my old grocery store for a while. It was an Alpha Beta Market in a shopping center not far from my old apartment. I remember going to the Alpha Beta one night and getting a copy of *The World According to Garp* by John Irving. On another occasion I bought a copy of *The Way the Future Was* by Frederick Pohl.

In 1980 or so I finished paying off the car loan on the Pinto and I wanted to get something special with the extra money I had each month. One thing I got was a compact stereo at Sears. It had a cassette deck, a turntable, and a receiver. It was a very basic stereo.

Later on a store called The Federated came to Fresno and opened a store on Blackstone. I loved the way electronic equipment smelled when I went into the store. I bought a good stereo system that included a Vector Research receiver, a tape deck, and some good speakers.

When I got home I kept having problems getting sound from the speakers. I took back the first receiver and got a replacement. I had the same problem with the second receiver and took it back. The problem was being caused by fuses shorting out. When wires crossed the wrong way fuses would short and you didn't get any sound.

I guess it was inevitable I would get someone complaining my stereo was too loud. One night I was playing some Emmylou Harris. I remember the song "Beneath Still Waters" was playing when some guy knocked on the door and claimed the stereo was too loud.

I was watching *Monday Night Football* when Howard Cosell announced that John Lennon had been shot and killed as he was coming home to his apartment in the Dakota in New York City. Lennon had just finished a recording session.

By that time I already lived through the assassination of President Kennedy, the murder of Dr. Martin Luther King, and the assassination of Senator Robert Kennedy.

Life went more or less routinely over the next few years. In 1982 Janet Headrick told us that her husband was getting transferred to Atlanta, Georgia, so she would be moving to Georgia. Janet was not only my supervisor, but my friend, so I found the news disheartening.

Pat Thompson replaced Janet as the supervisor. I thought briefly I might get some consideration for the job, but Pat had a lot more seniority and Ken Forsyth had a grudge because I had turned down the job in Sandy Wolfe's department earlier.

Pat's management style was totally different than Janet's. Janet was decisive and Pat never appeared comfortable making a decision. Her solution to any sensitive matter was to "ask Ken."

By the time she became Disbursement supervisor Pat was divorced. She never talked about her ex-husband in the first person. She always referred to him as "the kids' dad." Every day when she left for lunch she made a joke about Robert Redford calling her.

I didn't care for Pat's management style and I resented the fact I didn't get promoted. I tried to upgrade my wardrobe and find a way to move to a different job.

I finally succeeded in getting a loan processor position in the Loan Agent Department.

The loan agents were quasi-loan officers. They solicited business, did a lot of prequalifying of prospective borrowers, and got paid on commission. I remember Dick Grill, who liked to play the naughty older man and who was a big Fresno State basketball fan, and Bob Zackney. You frequently heard Bob Zackney on the phone spelling his name Z-A-C-K-N-E-Y.

One time I was talking about President Franklin Roosevelt and Bob Zackney was nearby and said, "Boo." Then I said something and he said he wasn't going to argue with me.

In 1984 the Oakland Raiders, my favorite team, were in the Super Bowl against the Washington Redskins. Bob Zackney bet on the Redskins and my friend Ray Pena and I bet on the Raiders. The Raiders won.

Another agent was a guy named Bud Alexander. Bud seemed out of his element and I regret that I was pretty critical of him. Work just gets frustrating sometimes.

A couple of women who came into the department had an impact on my life. Marie Benavides was a fiery lady who was immensely likable most of the time, but difficult to deal with when she got upset about something. Karen Builta had moved down from Washington State and Karen's major interest in life was men.

Marie began lobbying me to date Karen. Karen and I didn't date much because we didn't share common interests and I was too much of a Puritan to feel comfortable with Karen's more relaxed views of sex and sexuality. I remember having lunch at a restaurant and Karen's chair tipped back and dumped her on the floor.

Karen talked a lot about her "bubble bath" photo, but I never saw it.

After it became obvious that Karen and I were not going to be a couple she and Marie started clubbing. Karen met a guy named Moe and that didn't work out because Moe was abusive and reportedly sold drugs.

She dated a guy named Greg. He was stationed at the Naval Air Station in Lemoore. He came into the office one day and struck me as a total boor. I think that relationship also broke up.

I had periodic conflicts with Marie. Karen told me that Marie had said I was a "weak man," which upset me. Then the feud was on for a while.

Karen and Marie liked going to events such as Chippendale's, the male stripper show, and I found that offensive.

I started job hunting and American Savings and Loan called me for an interview. I talked to a guy named Bob Garavelo and I felt like I had been mugged. Guarantee was more specialized in its loan processing procedures than other savings and loans, so I wasn't familiar with some of the details Mr. Garavelo asked me about.

Strangely enough, I got a job offer anyway as a funding clerk. My instincts were to decline the job because I didn't like Garavelo. But I was unhappy at Guarantee because of the situation with Karen Builta and Marie and because the pay was pretty low. So I accepted the job offer at American Savings.

It didn't take long to realize I had made a mistake. Garavelo was arrogant and had the attitude that it was "my way or the highway" in dealing with other people in the real estate lending industry. I wanted to go back to Guarantee.

I contacted Pam Edwards, who was managing the agent department, and I got rehired at Guarantee.

Pam Edwards got promoted to head the administration department and I eventually moved there. My job was to be a contact with the branch offices, to write memos, and to write procedures and maintain procedures manuals. I was also supervisor for a couple of people.

There were several manuals to be maintained and the whole system was inefficient. I thought that maybe using memos as updates to manuals might work and sent out a memo to get reactions. I got shot down.

The biggest problem was dealing with Sandy Wolfe. Sandy had been in charge of writing procedures for a long time and she was very territorial

Pam was concerned that Sandy would retire and she said Sandy had a vast store of knowledge that we couldn't afford to lose.

To illustrate how petty Sandy could be: I sent out a memo using the word "confirm" in the sense of "verifying." She sent a comment to me complaining about the use of the word "confirm." I began to feel like I was dealing with an entrenched bureaucracy.

I had to learn how to calculate annual percentage rates using a financial calculator. Guarantee was testing out a new software program to calculate A.P.R.'s and Pam Edwards wanted to me to verify the program was calculating correctly.

One problem we encountered with some interest rates--if they were a little unusual--is that the loan officers didn't have tables showing the payment. They would round the payment up to the next highest rate listed in the interest rate tables. When the computer system calculated the payment it was different, of course.

I was interested in finding the equation that would allow the payment to be calculated correctly. I found the way to calculate the correct payment on the financial calculator and I sent out a memo explaining the method. Then one of the management people sent a note indicating he was skeptical of my method, which I knew was absolutely correct.

Someone else who didn't understand the way variable loans worked was a guy named John Dickey. Mr. Dickey was in management, but I don't recall his exact title.

He called me one day to complain about the A.P.R. that was calculated on a loan for a Guarantee employee. The employee was getting an adjustable loan. Mr. Dickey apparently didn't understand that variable loans were calculated on a worst case scenario. For example, if the loan terms allowed the interest rate to increase 5%, then the A.P.R. would be calculated on that adjusted rate because we had no way of knowing what the future interest rate would be.

I liked getting to travel to other branches now and then. I visited the Bakersfield office, the Visalia office, and the Merced office and the people were always nice to me.

One of my worst experiences in administration was having to give a presentation before some people from the branch offices one day. Public speaking terrifies me and I didn't rival Winston Churchill that day.

I didn't like the bureaucracy. A woman named Wildon Cutts was the supervisor for the loan processors who weren't in the agent department. She wasn't very flexible on much of anything. There was a guy named Woody Claussen who had been associated with Guarantee for years and he was gruff and close-minded. I found it increasingly difficult to deal with Sandy Wolfe and Pam Edwards didn't want to alienate Sandy.

A new savings and loan called Financial Savings and Loan was starting and a friend named Ray Pena knew the supervisors at Financial Savings. Ray had worked in the agent department at Guarantee before he changed jobs. When I talked to the people at Financial Savings it seemed like it would be a good move.

FINANCIAL SAVINGS AND LOAN

I accepted a job as a funding clerk at Financial Savings. Their office was just down the street on Shaw Avenue. The office was new when I first went there. There weren't even cubicles and you could still smell the new carpet glue.

There wasn't much business in the first few weeks. I was trying to learn quadratic equations from an algebra class I was taking at Fresno City College and I occupied myself with those to keep busy.

The funding procedure was different from what I had experienced at Guarantee Savings. Financial Savings worked a lot with brokers, for instance. Brokers, instead of loan officers, did much of the preliminary work to qualify buyers for loans. Then loan officers at Financial Savings would complete the process.

I had to type checks instead of preparing the checks on a computer and the part of the job that created the most problems for me was making a "copy file." A copy file was photocopies we kept of the file. We sent the original file to the main office in San Diego, California.

Having to make copy files always kept me behind. One day when making copy files it occurred to me I might have enough savings to survive a few months if I quit. So I gambled and quit Financial Savings in May, 1987.

Then I had my first exposure to temporary agencies and temporary jobs. The first temp job I got was at Fireman's Fund Insurance on Shaw Avenue. I typed pages for insurance policies. This was typing on an old-fashioned typewriter, not a word processor. The job was supposed to last for six months, but lasted around six weeks.

I had a data entry job in downtown Fresno and one afternoon I was headed home. I was stopped at a red light in front of the new jail that was being constructed. When the light changed I felt a bump. I pulled into a parking place just up the street.

A Fresno city bus was at the intersection. My car had apparently had some contact with the bus.

When the bus pulled up they said I had bumped into the bus. I am still skeptical that was true, but I couldn't disprove what they said. A passenger on the bus claimed that he had suffered a whiplash injury.

I'm not a physicist, but I doubt he was injured. The contact was so minimal and my car was so much smaller than the bus I doubt there was enough force to cause any injures. The damage to my car was so minimal that I had a hard time seeing it. But the guy was put into a neck brace and transported to the hospital. My insurance company paid him $1,300.

About a year later a process server showed up at my door. The guy was suing me and the City of Fresno. I was extremely angry because I thought the initial claim was a sham and now he was trying to extract more money. I wrote to a columnist for the Fresno *Bee* named Jim Wasserman about the case.

Mr. Wasserman came to my apartment to interview me. He liked what I had written to the City of Fresno: "If justice prevails in the universe, all lawyers will wind up in hell." He used that quote in his column a few days later.

My insurance company threatened sanctions against the guy suing me, his attorney dropped the case, and the City paid him $300.

Ironically, that same year I got a jury summons. I asked for a postponement because I had just started a new job.

One of the worst aspects of doing temporary jobs for me was trying to find the location of the assignment. This was in the days prior to GPS technology, so I had to try to use a map and directions that the temp agency gave me.

I had problems finding WestAir Airlines, for example. Later on I got a job with WestAir, but the first day I had a problem. The absolute worst was an assignment with the Fresno City Hall. I searched and searched until I finally found the office. The job itself was fairly stressful. It involved taking lots of phone calls and transferring the calls to the appropriate people, who usually wouldn't pick up the call. Then I had to take messages.

WESTAIR AIRLINES

Right around that time I interviewed with WestAir Airlines for a job in their Revenue Accounting Department. WestAir offered me a job as a pricing clerk at $4.90 an hour on the evening shift. It was considerably less money than I had made at Financial Savings and Loan, but an airline job appealed to me.

I went to work at 4 p. m. and got off at 12:30 a. m. I liked the hours because I am a night person. I worked with a lady named Dee Hall, a couple of other ladies, and a guy named Robert Vargas.

My job was to determine the portion of fares that belonged to WestAir Airlines. The routes were set up on a wheel and spoke system. For example, a trip might go from Fresno to San Francisco to Seattle. The Fresno to San Francisco part of the trip was handled by WestAir ("lifted" in the trade) and WestAir collected a prorated amount of the fare for the Fresno-San Francisco "lift."

WestAir's flights connected to United Airlines. WestAir and United Airlines negotiated prorates about every three months.

About the first thing I did when I reported to work each afternoon was to tape a piece of paper to my desk. We used the paper to keep the carbon from the tickets from transferring to the desk surface. We used purple pens to write the prices on the tickets. Purple was one of the colors allowed by the airline accounting departments.

I learned about point-to-point fares (such as a trip starting in Fresno and stopping in San Francisco) and about fares collected in Canadian dollars. I started to learn the various airport codes ("FAT" for Fresno). Some tickets didn't have agreed prorates and we had to use a computer system called "PIPPS" to get the prorates.

Robert Vargas and a lady named Pearl were so-called "lifter sorters." Most nights Robert didn't seem too interested in working. He liked to listen to a local pop music station. I'll always associate Fleetwood Mac music with those days.

We worked in a long narrow building that was a former military barracks and you could hear planes outside. The WestAir hangar was nearby and mechanics serviced the aircraft there. Most of the planes when I started were small "Bandits." They carried 15-20 passengers.

When I heard airplane engines I felt a strange sense of romance. Occasionally, we saw a ticket used by someone famous. I saw connections to foreign destinations like Paris or London. There were lots of connections to Hawaii. I still have a fondness for the scent of jet fuel.

The person who trained me when I first started was a lady named Maureen Edwards. Maureen always seemed distant to me and I struggled at first learning to price tickets. But I gradually caught on and pricing seemed like second nature.

The data entry department also worked an evening shift. For some reason, there was friction between the pricing department and the data entry department. A woman named Dawn in the data entry department always seemed ready to jump down your throat.

I also crossed swords with a woman named Joy.

After working for a while in the long barracks-like building, the Revenue Accounting Department moved to a trailer on the side of the main building. One night when we were working in the trailer a WestAir plane was having trouble deploying its landing gear. Maureen Edwards was there and forbade us going outside to see the plane land.

The plane landed successfully in a shower of sparks. WestAir had a few bizarre incidents in those days such as planes landing at the wrong airport.

After we worked in the trailer for a while, we moved to a ramshackle building just a little distance away. I remember some of the women employees complaining incessantly about the bathroom being dirty. The data entry department also moved and worked in the room next door to the pricing department.

I got promoted to supervisor of the evening shift. Having some recognition and more money was good. Having to supervise was bad. A few people I remember causing me problems: a guy named Raul, a woman named Donna, and another woman named Jennifer. There was a quiet guy named Rafael. Rafael was Filipino and sometimes the cultural differences created problems. Another woman named Michelle worked on the evening shift and we usually got along.

Luke was one of the most interesting people on the night shift. Luke was a young guy whose mother had died years before. His father worked for the local Mercedes dealership. You didn't have to be around Luke for long until you found out his heroes were Dan Fielding, the lecherous character in the television show "Night Court," and George Thorogood, whose song "I Drink Alone" was often cited by Luke. But for all of that Luke was pretty much a straight arrow and very good at pricing airline tickets.

A couple of running themes I developed with Luke were his list of clichés and the people he was said to resemble. One teacher at Fresno City College said that Luke looked like football quarterback Doug Flutie.

One time Luke was talking about how he thought he would look good wearing a Speedo. I said, "Some guys would look good in a Speedo, Luke, but you're not one of them."

Another running commentary from Luke was how much money he had saved. His goal, which he ultimately achieved, was to get a college degree.

On Halloween WestAir allowed people to dress in costume and there was a contest for the best costume. Luke won one year when he dressed as Gumby. He used the same costume the next year, but it didn't work the second time.

Some of the things I remember from the WestAir days: the execution of convicted serial killer Ted Bundy in Florida, the riots in Los Angeles after the policemen accused of beating Rodney King were acquitted, and the 1989 earthquake that inflicted heavy damage on the Bay Area and delayed the World Series.

Just about everyone who worked at WestAir listened to the radio to try to get through the drudgery of another shift. Back around 1989 I listened to radio dramas played on KMJ radio in the evening and to non-political talk shows. I remember they played Progresso Soup commercials incessantly. For some reason, I was fascinated by the Ted Bundy case on the night before he was executed.

Later on in 1989 we had a major earthquake. It was later named the Loma Prieta earthquake. I felt the rocking in the old building where we worked, but there was no damage. I had cable TV back then, including a San Francisco station, and I went home that night and watched some of the earthquake coverage.

I bought my first VCR at Montgomery Ward in 1988 and I used the VCR extensively because I was at work in the evening. I remember taping "The Tonight Show" when Johnny Carson said farewell.

One winter night Luke and I decided to go out for our lunch break. His windshield was frosted over and rather than wait for the windshield to defrost he took off. He had a view that looked like a pinprick to me.

I had the most hassles with a woman named Donna. Donna was a few years older than me and, from hearing her talk, it sounded like she was working all the time. But she was forever changing her schedule and not working her normally assigned hours. She was also one of those people who went to management to complain about allegedly being treated unfairly.

Daphne was an interesting character. Daphne was intelligent and extremely fast at pricing. Sometimes she made more mistakes because she was going so fast. She liked *The Brady Bunch* and Mickey Mouse watches.

A woman named Jan started as a temporary employee and then got hired. At first I thought Jan would be a really good employee. But she developed an attitude. The thing that bothered me was how she wanted to "tattle" on other people. When I mentioned that on her review she was enraged. Needless to say, doing performance reviews was not a favorite activity.

Another woman who worked as a temporary employee was Marika. Marika was pretty and vivacious and actually a pretty good worker. But she wasn't good at arriving at work on time and that probably cost her a chance at being hired permanently. I remember a couple of things about Marika.

One night I said something about jalapeno peppers increasing your metabolism and helping you to lose weight. Marika promptly ate too many jalapenos and got an upset stomach.

On another night Michelle and I got into a discussion about religion with Marika. Michelle and I were both skeptical about religion and Marika felt she was being ganged up on when we got into a debate. I still feel bad that she was upset.

The supervisor for a long time was Mary Stanley. I liked Mary, but she missed work a great deal. When it's a supervisor missing work it makes it difficult to accomplish much.

When Maureen Edwards left the company a guy named Raul Fernandes came in as manager of Revenue Accounting. Raul changed some procedures and it seemed from that point on we had unending overtime. I finally stopped working Saturdays because I was on salary and I didn't get paid for overtime.

Mary Stanley was eventually replaced by a guy named Kevin Alexander. Kevin had worked with Raul Fernandes before and Raul advertised Kevin as a tough guy who would bring some discipline into the department.

I was a little troubled on Kevin's first day when he priced some tickets and did them totally wrong. As time went on, I never understood what qualifications he really possessed to be in management. Any time I talked to him about problems in the department his response was, "We'll play it by ear."

I dreamed for years about visiting Key West, Florida. As a Hemingway fan, I had a major interest in Key West. Hemingway had lived there and done some of his best work there. So in 1990 I decided to make the trip.

As an airline employee, I probably could have flown for a reduced fare. But it would also have meant flying standby, which could be a major hassle. So I decided to fly on standby from Fresno to San Francisco and then fly regular fare from San Francisco to Key West.

A friend in the Bay Area was renting a boat and she said I could sleep that night on the boat. Pat picked me up at the airport and we went to Carl's Jr. for dinner. She dropped me off at the boat and she went to stay the night at a friend's house.

There wasn't a TV on the boat, but there was a radio and I listened to the radio a good part of the evening. When I stepped out of the boat I could see the hills surrounding San Francisco and the lights looked like jewels.

The next morning Pat picked me up and took me the airport. I boarded the American Airlines flight from San Francisco to Dallas. A guy who directed aircraft on the ground, called a marshaller, twirled his stick like a drum major leading a parade before we took off. Some of the most exciting words of my life were when the pilot said, "Flight attendants, please prepare for takeoff."

We climbed above the fog and the fog was tinged with gold from the morning sun. I flew all the way from San Francisco and landed in Dallas. When I was walking through the Dallas airport I had to dodge those golf carts they use to transport people through the terminal. After my layover I boarded a plane for Miami.

Instead of a movie, they showed CNN News on the Miami flight. The pilot pointed out the Everglades as we flew over. As we were landing in Miami the Concord jet was also coming in.

I didn't have much time before my Key West flight was scheduled to depart and I scrambled to find the correct gate and get on the plane. I made it in the nick of time and fell in love with the beautiful turquoise water in the Gulf Stream as we flew to Key West.

When we landed Key West was quiet. Maybe it was because I had been on airplanes all day, but the quiet was welcome. When I walked outside an old van was there and the guy evidently provided taxi service. I needed a ride to the Holiday Inn.

I rode the van to the Holiday Inn and paid the guy and he wasn't offering to give me change. He looked seriously at me and I figured the extra money was a tip and I let it go.

I made arrangements for my room and went to the Hemingway Café for dinner. I had fettuccini alfredo and swordfish and, to emulate how Hemingway would express it, I was never happier.

That night the Orioles were playing the White Sox on WGN TV. Ben McDonald, who was once considered a top pitching prospect, was pitching for the Orioles.

The next morning I woke up fairly early and decided I would walk to Whitehead Street to see Hemingway's house. It was within fairly easy walking distance, or so I thought. I wasn't counting on the intense July humidity and I wore boots.

I arrived at the Hemingway house before they officially opened, but they opened shortly thereafter. I was already wrung out from the July heat. I could understand why Hemingway didn't spend his summers in Key West.

I took the tour of the house. I heard about the descendants of Hemingway's cats. The cats are noted for being polydactyl, having an extra toe. One cat was named Mae West because of the way she walked. I went upstairs to the bedroom and saw a reproduction of a cat sculpture Pablo Picasso had done for Hemingway. The sculpture was chained to the wall in case anyone had ideas of taking it.

We were told of Hemingway's rage when his second wife, Pauline Pfeiffer, built a swimming pool. Ernest allegedly threw down a penny and said she was spending his last cent for construction of the pool.

My favorite part of the tour was seeing Ernest's studio up above the pool. There were security bars in place and I couldn't go inside the studio. But I could see a work table with a typewriter. Full book shelves lined the walls. Trophies from Hemingway's big game hunts were mounted on the walls.

I went to a book store and looked for a book by Walter Tevis, who wrote *The Hustler.* The guy in the store didn't seem to know about Walter Tevis. He mentioned that Anne Rice, author of several vampire novels, once wrote porn. I bought a copy of a book by Tom McGuane.

It wasn't a long walk back to the Holiday Inn, but it felt like a long walk because the humidity sapped me. When I went out the next few days I used the Conch Tour Train. The station was just across the street from the motel.

There was a service across the street that could fly you to the Dry Tortugas, but I couldn't afford it. There was also a souvenir shop and I bought a small bell and a box of seashells.

Later on I went out on a glass bottom boat and got to see schools of tropical fish and nurse sharks. I went by the newer version of Sloppy Joe's Bar. The original Sloppy Joe's was a Hemingway hangout. I remember a band playing the Santana song "Black Magic Woman."

Early one morning there was a booming sound like the sound of artillery. It was a Key West thunderstorm and featured the loudest thunder I've ever heard.

I liked the briny, mildewed, tropical scent of Key West. When I was on the plane flying out of the city I remember thinking, "Goodbye, Key West. I hope I will see you again someday."

I didn't really stop to think about how geopolitical events were going to impact WestAir or my life. Trouble was brewing in the Middle East and the Middle East meant oil and effects on oil prices. Jet fuel is the single largest expense for an airline and problems with Saddam Hussein and Iraq were driving up the price of oil and jet fuel.

On the night the first Gulf War started people in Revenue Accounting had their radios turned up way too loud, but I didn't make an issue of it. You heard about the launch of Scud missiles by the Iraqis and you wondered about Saddam Hussein's boasts about the "mother of all battles."

I talked to Luke and he was concerned about the war, but there was little doubt the United States and the so-called coalition forces would defeat Iraq.

WestAir had launched an east coast airline called Atlantic Coast Airlines. There was also a subsidiary in the Pacific Northwest called NPA. ACA helped save WestAir for a time when the company began drowning in red ink. ACA was sold for much needed cash.

But because WestAir was having financial troubles it became an attractive takeover target. The company merged with New Mexico based Mesa Airlines in 1992.

The CEO at Mesa Airlines was a guy named Larry Risley. Risley liked to boast about his business skills. He wrote a series of letters to the people at WestAir. One of the first things he said was that he would discontinue the use of the word "associates" to describe us. We were officially back to being employees.

He also announced that a guy from Mesa named Jonathan Ornstein would become company president at WestAir. He instituted a new dress code. We had been allowed to dress fairly casually up until that point, but we had to dress more formally under Mr. Risley's rules. He decreed that people with offices had to keep their office doors open.

I didn't like his arrogance and I wrote him a letter. I wouldn't write the letter today, but things seemed to be headed in a very oppressive direction and I thought he should know about that. One of the things I suggested was wearing uniforms if the company was so concerned with a dress code.

One of the worst changes was having to work in the day time instead of the swing shift I had worked for about five years. I started working a shift from 7 a. m. to 3:30 p. m.

Mesa installed a Muzak system and we listened to elevator music all day. We had to worry about being laid off. I remember going to work in the afternoon when I was still going in the afternoons and wondering if I would learn about a layoff that day. They kept us in suspense for some time.

Mesa also constructed a new building. We had to go through a security gate to get to the building.

For several years I had a running feud of sorts with a guy named Mark. He was a major Rush Limbaugh fan and I kept hearing those "gems" of wisdom spouted by Limbaugh every day on KMJ Radio. One of Mark's favorites was about "punishing the achievers" if you required the affluent to pay a higher percentage of taxes.

Mark was a lapsed Mormon. He grew his hair long so that it hung around his shoulders and when he first started at WestAir he drove an old Pinto. Later on, it seemed he was always asking people for rides.

One afternoon after we got off from work I got into a long conversation with Mark. Later on, Luke asked me if Mark was a little long-winded. From that moment on we called Mark "The Long-Winded Guy."

Mark took special pride in what he considered his mastery of Microsoft Excel. Every three months WestAir negotiated new prorates with United Airlines and it was Mark's job to assemble the prorates into a worksheet that could be passed out to the pricers in Revenue Accounting. I had the job of proofreading his work.

One of the people in the data entry department was a guy named Harry. Harry was a flaming homosexual. I have nothing against gay people, but he still made me uncomfortable. Amazingly, Harry had served in the military (the Air Force, I think) and he was a right-wing conservative.

One day just to irritate me he brought in a Rush Limbaugh bumper sticker, which I promptly tore apart. An aggrieved Harry told me, "Hey, I had to work hard to get that."

Another guy in Revenue Accounting was Sean. Sean liked to talk like a conservative, but I'm not sure he really understood all the implications.

When Newt Gingrich and the Republicans concocted their "Contract With America" and won big in the congressional elections in 1994 Mark, Sean, and others were ecstatic. At home someone piled several copies of *The Fresno Bee* in the apartment complex laundry room with the big page one headlines about the Republican victories. I rewrote the headlines to say things like, "The Working Class Loses."

It was around 1994 or 1995 that Jonathan Ornstein moved on to another Mesa-owned airline and a guy named Rolly Bergeson took over as company president. Bergeson was fond of sending out letters to WestAir employees and apparently had a bad relationship with the pilots' union. Someone referred to Bergeson's letters as "Rolly Grams."

Bergeson announced that many of us would have our salaries frozen, including me. I wrote him a letter and asked what my incentive was supposed to be for doing a good job. No matter what I did, I wouldn't get a raise. Proving himself a hypocrite, Larry Risley took a handsome bonus, something like $1.5 million, for himself.

Kevin Alexander essentially ambushed me over my letter to Bergeson. He even complained about letters I had written to *The Fresno Bee*. I wrote *The*

Bee frequently about politics, but I said nothing about WestAir.

I raised the point that I didn't think a raise of $400-$500 a year was going to impact the company very much and Mr. Alexander's response was, "What if everybody got that?" It still astonishes me. He was essentially saying you weren't supposed to get compensated for doing your job well.

On another occasion I knew I couldn't pay my rent if I got my paycheck on the scheduled payday. The company had an arrangement where you could get paid early if you were going to be out for some reason such as vacation. I asked my supervisor if I could put in a request to get my paycheck a little earlier. If I didn't pay my rent on time, I would get hit with a late charge.

WestAir's paychecks were issued every two weeks and this particular payday occurred after my rent was due. My supervisor approved my request. Then the day I was expecting to get the check I heard that Rolly Bergeson was putting a hold on it. It was supposedly outside of company policy. I called him and explained my problem, but he wasn't helpful. I still managed to get the check, but the whole incident was emblematic of the way management was treating us.

On December 14, 1994, I was having lunch in my car when I saw smoke billowing into the sky. When I went back into the office someone told me a plane had crashed. It was a private jet that was participating in a military exercise. The crew members and one person on the ground were killed. The pilot reportedly took extraordinary steps to avoid crashing into a school and the plane crashed in the middle of Olive Avenue in the Tower District.

As 1995 began Fresno had lots and lots of rain. My Mustang didn't handle rain well. When I was driving to work one January morning I hit a patch of water that splashed up into the engine. When I stopped for a red light at Ashlan and Winery the car died.

I managed to get it started once or twice, but then it died and I couldn't get it to start. Two guys offered me help me push the car out of the way

As they pushed I saw some headlights coming from the opposite direction. I naively thought the other driver would see my car and stop. Instead, she slammed into the rear of the car on the passenger side. I was thrown into the windshield and I cut my forehead and got a black eye.

So I was suddenly without a car. I bought a Hyundai Excel in the next couple of days, but I was faced with a car payment again.

That summer I heard about a postal service regional encoding center that was going to open in Selma. I decided to take the test.

The test involved both the usual written civil service test and a typing test. I did reasonably well on the typing test. When we were taking the written exam I was folding the book over to make it easier for me to handle when a jerk who was monitoring the test grabbed the book from me and slammed it back down on the desk. Even now I wish I had just stood up and walked out.

I passed the test and got invited to an interview. One thing they hadn't mentioned in their job ad was that you had to pass a physical. Somehow I managed to pass the physical, including the eye exam.

I had reservations about the job. For one thing, it was a temporary job. You worked as a temp for a year and then, in theory, you were hired to work as a temp for another year. You also had to get through a week's training successfully, or you weren't hired. The guy who interviewed me said that many good typists didn't survive the week.

What influenced me more than anything else to give my resignation to WestAir was yet another new Mesa policy. You didn't get paid your accrued vacation if you didn't give two them a two-week notice. If I waited until I was sure I had the post office job, I would forfeit my vacation pay.

The first days I worked at the post office I still worked at WestAir. Things seemed to be going well. But after the weekend things took a turn for the worse. They called the job data entry, but it was far more demanding than a typical data entry job.

The job was to enter appropriate information to spray bar codes on mail as it was being processed. You saw an image on the computer screen and entered the code. One of the problems that occurred was what they called "double fed." It was when two pieces of mail got stuck together instead of completing their trip through the post office machinery.

For some reason I just couldn't recognize the double fed mail and that and other things caused me to fall irrevocably behind.

One of the things that amazed me about the post office was how the supervisors didn't work. They stood around and watched other people work.

After a week I washed out of the post office job and I was unemployed for the first time in several years. I couldn't afford an apartment anymore and my Mom graciously let me move into her apartment.

MISSION FOODS

I took a battery of tests at various temporary agencies. I started a fairly long temp job in late October or early November in the Corporate Credit Department of Gottschalks Department Store for the Christmas holidays.

Gottschalks had been around for decades and they apparently beefed up their staffing every Christmas season with temporary employees.

I got a call from the temp agency while I was still asleep. I dressed in a hurry and hustled over to the Gottschalks headquarters that was located near Woodward Park. We assembled in the break room. The boss said we were restricted in where we could park and I had to move my car to a different location. We were also informed that the company had famous or prominent clients and we had to guard their information. One client was pop star Michael Jackson. Another was Fresno mayor Jim Patterson.

The job involved taking calls from the Gottschalks stores when the customer was "over limit" or other problems. One procedure I thought was crazy was having the person in the store read a credit card number that we didn't bother to write down. It was all a show for the customer on the other end.

When things got slack we had to file. Filing isn't the most desirable job anyway, but especially when everything is jammed so tightly into the filing cabinet that you don't have any room.

We had to ask permission to go on breaks or to go to lunch. When the call volume got high someone would shout out about how high the call volume was. I'm not sure how we were supposed to handle that. If a store called and a customer was exceeding their credit line, we had to shout out "Over limit!" and wait for a supervisor to handle the situation.

What I remember most about those days was listening to Chick Hearn describe the Lakers games on the radio on my way home. Shaquille O'Neal had recently joined the Lakers and I was rooting for a championship.

One day at lunch I talked briefly to a woman in distress. She had been laid off from another job and was working as a temp for Gottschalks too. It didn't appear to be going well. She said something about, "These companies have got us by the throat."

I wasn't really sorry when the Gottschalks assignment ended. I put in a token job application and asked for $7.50 an hour. I knew that Gottschalks probably wouldn't want to pay even that pittance.

The next temp job I got was a data entry job with Vendo. Vendo was a Fresno-based company that manufactured vending machines. I had to go through a security checkpoint to get into the complex and I worked in a trailer that was inside a warehouse.

The supervisor hadn't mentioned that I would have to work the weekend too, but I agreed. When I was there I wasn't sure why they hired me because I wound up with lots of idle time.

I was in the warehouse with another office employee one day when one of the warehouse workers sounded hostile. He said something derogatory and said "even temps" were included. I don't know if he was kidding.

I moved on to a job at Table Mountain Casino. It was for data entry and it was in a trailer again. I was also back to filing at first. I didn't like the supervisor much. When I got to do data entry things went better.

When I went through the filing I kept seeing events Table Mountain had featured events such as martial arts fighting.

Table Mountain is known for having good food at cheap prices. But employees weren't permitted to eat in the dining room. Employees also weren't supposed to park in the front parking lot.

My first day I parked behind the building. I had to park on a slope. I had just started to learn to use a standard transmission and I ran into a problem when I was getting ready to leave for the day.

Someone had parked fairly close behind me and when I let off the clutch the car started to roll. I never made contact with the car behind me. I used my emergency brake to keep the car from rolling and managed to squeeze out of the parking place. I pulled into an area to turn around when suddenly a security guard blocked my way with his truck.

Someone from inside Table Mountain thought I had crashed into the car behind me and they called security. Two management types came from inside the building and noted there was no damage to the car behind me and I left. The rest of my assignment with Table Mountain I parked in the front parking lot.

I got an assignment out near Selma and one morning I was waiting to make a right turn when a big rig truck driver turned his front wheel into the left rear fender of my car. He told his insurance company that I had not yielded to him when he was making a wide turn with his truck.

At first I pursued suing him in small claims court, but I ran into a paralegal who was either unethical or incompetent. He charged me $150 to file suit against the truck driver. When I finally got the papers to file the lawsuit I found everything was wrong and I wound up sending the papers to the truck driver myself.

The truck driver made loud noises about trouble he could cause me and I tried a different strategy. I went back to the scene of the accident and took a camera. I waited for a big rig to make a right turn at the intersection and I snapped a picture. I wanted to show that it wasn't necessary to make a wide turn and that the truck driver had turned from the wrong lane when he crashed into me.

I sent the photos to the truck driver's insurance company and showed them his account of the accident was a lie and they finally paid my claim.

I kept working temporary jobs and I got an assignment with Mission Foods. Mission Foods is a major Mexican foods manufacturer based in Monterrey,

Mexico. They had a plant out near the well-known Cherry Auction in Fresno.

Mission was owned by a man named Don Roberto. A portrait of Don Roberto was in the conference room and he reminded me of the Godfather.

My job was to process invoices sent in by Mission Foods distributors. They were independent contractors who sold Mission Foods products to stores. They were supposed to get signatures on invoices for credit accounts, collect money on cash accounts, and send the invoices and cash each day for us to process.

One of the most difficult parts of the job was reading handwritten invoices.

Most of the time distributors used a hand-held computer to print their invoices, but occasionally they did the hand-written variety. The other issue was getting credit invoices that weren't properly signed.   We had to hold those invoices.

One distributor in particular complained constantly that he wasn't paid correctly. But he also sent in lots of credit invoices without signatures. I started documenting the invoices in a section easy for him and management to see each week.

Another distributor held onto his cash instead of submitting it each day. He wound up owing the company lots of money and filed for bankruptcy.

The district managers didn't understand the accounting system and they were always complaining that accounting wasn't paying their distributors correctly. It was actually a fairly simple system.

The distributors were paid a commission based on the inventory they purchased. To settle their debt with the company they had to clear their inventory by writing credit invoices and submitting cash for their cash invoices. If they were diligent about submitting their invoices and submitting them properly, there were usually very few problems.

I was hired in June, 1996, and worked for some time at very low wages. A manager named Armando, who worked in the Los Angeles office, finally got me a raise to $10.50 an hour, which seemed like a fortune at the time. I was able to get an apartment.

At Mission Foods I felt a little like a traveler to a foreign country. Most of the people there spoke Spanish. Some people spoke only Spanish. When they had meetings there was someone to speak in Spanish and someone to speak in English.

When I first started, the accounting manager was a guy named Albert. Maria was the name of the supervisor. I worked with a couple of women clerks. One was named San Juana and the other clerk was also named Maria.

Later on, they hired a guy named Richard. Richard's big ambition was to move to Bakersfield and become the SAC (Settlement Accounting Clerk) there. But he got arrested and thrown into jail and that ended his job at Mission. On one occasion Richard acted like he wanted to fight me for allegedly taking his chair.

I had been using an old hard back chair because my office chair was broken. One morning an office chair was by my desk. I had no idea how it got there. Richard assumed it was his chair and assumed that I had taken it.

It surprised me a little that he liked to listen to country music. I remember hearing Martina McBride on his radio. I listened to a lot of sports talk radio back in those days.

The work at Mission was inconsistent. On Mondays and Tuesdays I was usually overloaded with work. Then it would tail off and the days were very long the rest of the week. Armando kept saying we were "overstaffed."

We didn't feel overstaffed after I came back from one vacation. Richard had been arrested and thrown into jail. San Juana was on vacation. Maria the clerk had gone on an emergency trip to Mexico. I and two temps had to get the work out.

Armando and a lady named Mary Taketani came up from Los Angeles to help us out. I put some work to the side that wasn't absolutely essential, such as filing, so we could concentrate on the more important issues. When San Juana returned from vacation she complained about the incomplete filing.

Later, after Armando had left the company, someone in Los Angeles decided we should run a calculator tape on the invoices to see that the total matched what the computer showed. But we ran out of calculator tape and the company was cutting back on supplies. I began adding the invoices without a calculator tape and then noting the total. Then San Juana complained about *that.*

Then we began to hear talk of a new accounting program called SAP. We had previously used a system called AS/400. The big advantage of SAP was that it was faster than AS/400. I should have seen the writing on the wall.

I still remember the day I got laid off. It was March 15, 2002. I was starting my morning routine when the Human Resources manager said she needed to see me. I went with her into the plant manager's office.

Instead of telling me I was laid off, he read a statement saying I was laid off. At first I didn't even comprehend what he was saying. Then the Human Resources manager asked if I would like a reference letter and I said yes. I was going to get some severance pay. I was told the decisions about layoffs were based on seniority and not on performance.

I boycotted Mission Foods for about ten years. I still feel it was a lousy way to treat me. They could have given me some notice they were planning a layoff. They did the same thing to some other people such as the lady who was the receptionist and the guy who handled the local IT issues. But any issues with Mission Foods paled in comparison to the jobs over the next ten years.

ALLIED INSPECTIONS

I answered an ad for a data entry job and got invited for an interview. The job was with a company called Allied Inspections. Their office was on First Street just a little way from the Fashion Fair Mall.

I first spoke to a woman named Lamona Forbes. She told me that Allied was a family business and did insurance inspections all over the country. I wasn't familiar at all with the insurance inspections business. I was advised I would take a typing test.

A guy named Ron Forbes, who was Lamona's husband, set up the typing test and I did all right. I then interviewed with the company president, a guy named Larry Lewallen. Mr. Lewallen offered me the job and asked if I could start that day. I said it would be better if I could start the following Monday.

The following Monday I got introduced to Anthony. Anthony was working in the back office with Ron Forbes. They were doing the IT work for Allied Inspections. I began training on scanning photos.

Scanning photos was fairly simple and pretty boring. Hard copy reports came in from the field inspectors and they had photos attached to the reports. You took the photos off the report and scanned two or three at a time. You saved the photos under the control number on the report. You kept track of the time you started and how many photos you scanned.

Allied Inspections was very much into micromanagement. You basically had to account for every minute in your day, even though you already clocked in and out on a time clock.

I had to report almost every second of work I did. I would scan "x" number of photos. Later, after I learned data entry, I would post "x" number of reports. I rarely heard directly from upper management about anything. If Mr. Lewallen was unhappy, he delegated enforcement to the supervisor.

Ron Forbes and his wife Lamona were my primary management contacts.

Norma Ruiz (later Leyva) was the supervisor. Ron was loud and profane and occasionally racist.

One time I overheard a phone conversation Ron Forbes had with an insurance underwriter. He was extremely rude on the phone and when he hung up he said, "He has to be a raghead."

Allied Inspections only offered one week of paid vacation a year. They did offer a few sick days, which Mission Foods had not offered, but Mission had two weeks of paid vacation. I was on the verge of qualifying for three weeks of vacation when I was laid off at Mission Foods.

Allied Inspections was very much a family affair, but not in any warm, fuzzy Norman Rockwell kind of way. I would compare it more to the Corleone family in *The Godfather*.

The owners were Jan and Don Sharp. Don Sharp also operated a used car dealership. Larry Lewallen was the company president and his half-brother Ron Forbes was a vice-president. An elderly lady they called "Grandma" worked in the front office. She was Jan Sharp's mother and worked at Allied for some time after I started.

Don Sharp came in almost every day. He brought in mail. Jan Sharp was rarely around. When you saw her she was driving her Jaguar. She had Husky dogs and one time she brought the dogs inside the office in a baby stroller. She made her major appearance around Christmas to give us token gifts and sometimes a small Christmas bonus.

I rarely saw or spoke to Larry Lewallen. I would see him inside his glass-enclosed office when I walked by, but he didn't communicate with me. Sometimes I would see him when I was working back in Ron Forbes's office. He and Ron had a sometimes testy relationship. Ron considered himself a computer guru and I had the sense he had some disdain for Larry's comparative lack of computer knowledge.

One of many discouraging things about working at Allied was having to use a key to get into the restroom. They typically kept two keys up near the front desk. It seemed the keys were always getting lost or misplaced. I never understood why management didn't supply us with our own keys.

In the first few weeks at Allied I got to know a lady named Ann Cook. Ann was just biding time until she could get another job. She, Anthony, and I took walks on our breaks. She and Anthony both left Allied after I had been there about three weeks.

One morning, after I had been at Allied just a few weeks, Microsoft was doing software updates. I accepted the updates. A little while later Ron Forbes came out onto the floor and asked if we had accepted the updates. When I said I had he began to berate me. It was the first time I had ever been yelled at by a management person and I hated Allied intensely from that moment.

When I first started at Allied the company was expanding the office to add more cubicles. Business was growing and they were hiring more people. One afternoon the guys working on the cubicles needed to do something with my cubicle and I went into the break room to get out of their way. They said their work would take five or ten minutes.

While I was in the break room Larry Lewallen walked in and asked if I was on a break. I told him I was just waiting for the workers to finish my cubicle and he immediately wanted me to move to work at someone else's desk. I was getting paid $9.00 an hour and it was going to take five or ten minutes. I'll let you draw your own conclusions.

The break room itself was fairly Spartan. There were no vending machines. There were tables and cheap plastic chairs, a refrigerator, and a microwave. There was a sign above the sink telling people to wash their own dishes. We periodically heard that they were going to clean out the refrigerator and to take your stuff or lose it. I never stored anything in the refrigerator, so I never worried about it.

The job got harder as time went on. Management wanted the data entry and reviewing positions to be combined. Reviewers had to see if all the required photos were on the report, that there was a diagram that matched the way the house looked, to list all the conditions noted on the house, to complete a replacement cost if the report got a replacement cost, to contact the inspector if there was a question, and sometimes use software to draw a diagram from the hand-written diagram sent by the inspector. In short, it was a very difficult job.

Despite all that, Larry Lewallen continued to call the job "data entry."

I slogged along in the job at Allied until 2006 and watched lots of people come and go. Sometimes I would notice that someone just wasn't there anymore.

A lady named Gay had to start reviewing. Apparently, management wasn't happy with her production and one morning she came back to her desk, obviously getting ready to leave. I told her at least she wouldn't have to do reviewing anymore.

The worst account for me that Allied took was an account called Millennium. Millennium reports were always submitted as hard copy reports instead of being completed on the computer by the inspectors. Hard copy reports entailed a lot of extra work for the reviewers, but we were somehow supposed to meet the "goals" management arbitrarily decided we should meet.

The worst part of the Millennium reports was the diagram program. Someone thought it was clever to design an "all-inclusive" diagram program. Instead of drawing two levels of a two-level home, for instance, you would draw both levels at once. The problem was you had to omit sections that weren't part of a level. For example, if the second level didn't totally cover the first level, you had to draw part of the first level as a "wing." You could get into some pretty complicated scenarios.

Millennium people also loved to return reports. You would think you were rid of the thing and it would come back like a boomerang with some problem they perceived. When I did Millennium reports I found myself trying to anticipate what their own reviewers would consider a problem.

About the same time that Millennium reports became part of our misery at Allied, management came up with the idea of "goals." We got a goal for the number of reports they expected us to complete for the day. The goals were usually totally unrealistic. Far from inspiring me, the goals made me hate the job even more. I still hate the word "goal."

A friend named Christine left Allied on Columbus Day, 2004, for a better job and I took over a job Christine had done.

It involved naming and organizing digital photos sent by the inspectors. I did "photo duty" two or three times a week and reviewing the rest of the week.

In December, 2005, my brother Gary was hospitalized. I heard that he was expected to be discharged right around Christmas. Then I got the devastating news that he had died.

I had some accrued vacation, so I was able to use that time to aid in the funeral preparation and to attend Gary's funeral. I don't remember seeing any flowers or other acknowledgments from Allied. I got a sympathy card after I returned to work.

In the property inspections business things tend to slow in the winter months. Insurance companies are getting ready to create their year-end reports and the weather is bad in many parts of the country, so business slows.

In the early part of 2006 Allied management was going into a semi-panic mode because business was slow. On March 14 they laid off a long-time employee named Marilyn. They also laid off a friend named Linda. The following day I was laid off. All of us were over 50 years old. I don't think that was a coincidence.

Larry Lewallen let Lamona Forbes do his dirty work. She informed me I was being laid off.

I had mixed feelings about being laid off. I loathed the job at Allied, but being unemployed, especially when you're older, is unsettling. I applied at temporary employment agencies. Within a few days I got an assignment with Zurich Insurance in Fresno.

The lady at the temporary employment agency told me that Zurich had a "beautiful new office." The office was new, but I didn't think it was beautiful. Everything was locked down. You had to use a security card to go almost anywhere, even the restroom. It was cavernous and mostly artificially lighted.

When I first arrived they gave me a voluminous set of policies and procedures to read. I skimmed through that and mentioned that I had a little pen knife with me. The lady wanted me to take my little knife back to the car.

I was eventually shown to a cubicle with a lady who was supposed to train me. She was obviously not interested in training me. She mentioned at some point that maybe they could assign me to filing or data entry. I went to lunch and when I returned she had gone to a meeting without even advising me or telling me what I was supposed to do.

I did some miscellaneous things the rest of the day and that evening I got a call from the temp agency that I wouldn't return to Zurich the next day. I thought it was a pretty awful place to work, but it is still annoying to not even get a chance to prove what you can do.

Then I got an assignment from a different temp agency with a company called Inland Star Trucking. I was told that Inland Starr was close to Mission Foods, where I had worked some years before. I didn't feel it was that close when I actually drove there.

It was another place that was locked down. You had to get admitted by someone at the front of the building. I was assigned to a woman named Peggy. It was the worst work day of my life.

A woman named Debbie, who had worked at Allied Inspections, was also working as a temp at Inland Star. Debbie left Allied to try to sell Mary Kay Cosmetics and I guess that didn't work out.

Peggy asked if I wanted to work on the computer or watch her go through the routine. I usually prefer to watch the steps first, make notes, and then try to do work from my notes. I had the feeling she didn't like that.

As the day went on, things got worse for me. It seemed I could never get my notes arranged. When I tried to work on the computer with Peggy watching me she would say "No!" like you would say to a dog. It was really no surprise at the end of the day that they told me "call my agency," which is just a way of telling you that you won't be back. I still wish I had written the company president and told him about the lousy way I got treated.

My next assignment was with a company called So Fresh. So Fresh was a produce company. You dealt with bills of lading and things like that. The lady training me told me that the people at So Fresh were permanent temps (an oxymoron). You had to work every other Saturday for about a half day. You got almost no holidays.

The job itself seemed immensely complicated to me and it was dispiriting to have no prospect of the job ever getting better. I felt terrible about it, but I told So Fresh that it just wasn't going to work out.

Then I moved onto a true temporary job that was going to be two or three days with a health insurance company called Health Comp located in downtown Fresno near the railroad tracks. The job was to stuff envelopes.

It was easy, but it was a horrible job. On the first day we had to stand all day. I passed forms to a lady who assembled them into a packet that would be stuffed into an envelope. Some guy talked about how he and his friends liked to eat fertilized chicken eggs.

The next day one of the supervisors complained that the addresses weren't lined up properly with the windows in the envelopes. We had to go through a stack of envelopes and make sure everything lined up. But at least we got chairs. As we neared the end of the project, I was looking forward to the end of the assignment.

When I got home I had a contact from a different temp agency about a data entry job with a law firm downtown. I never have liked traveling to downtown Fresno, but a data entry job sounded more appealing than the other temp jobs I had suffered through.

The law firm job involved entering data about billable hours for attorneys into a database. It was the first temp job I had on this round that really fit me.

When I got home one day I had a surprise email from Norma at Allied

Inspections asking if I would be interested in returning to work at Allied. I definitely was conflicted. I loathed the job at Allied, but it seemed a better option than the temp jobs I had been doing. At least, in theory, it was more stable.

So I found myself back at Allied Inspections and wishing I could move on to something else.

It wasn't long before Larry Lewallen was demanding mandatory overtime on Saturdays again. I remember going to see Merle Haggard perform at The Fresno Fair on a Friday evening and realizing I would have to trudge into Allied the next morning.

As we approached Thanksgiving in 2007, things got interesting. I saw a blond woman around the office and I didn't know who she was. Then Larry Lewallen and Ron Forbes were suddenly attending lots of meetings.

After the series of meetings, I went into the office the next morning and saw that Ron Forbes was already there. He was there just a few minutes and as he was leaving he told someone, "See you."

Later that morning the staff got called to the front of the office. Jan Sharp was there along with the blond woman. The blond woman was Victoria Riddle, Larry Lewallen's sister.

She explained that Larry Lewallen and Ron Forbes had resigned and that she would be heading up the company. She intimated that Larry Lewallen and Ron Forbes had participated in unethical behavior, but she never specified what she meant.

The next day when I came into the office I found out that Jeremy Davis, the IT person, and Norma Ruiz, the supervisor, had both resigned. Victoria Riddle and her husband, Perry, would be running the company. They brought in an IT guy they knew named Matt Jones.

Early in her tenure Victoria Riddle tried to reach out to the employees. She came around in the morning and greeted us at our desks. She and her husband began offering gift cards to the reviewer who posted the most reports each day. They bought pizza for the office.

There was talk of developing a new website and I had some ideas that the Riddles seemed to like. I began working with one other person and with Matt Jones to develop the website.

We heard that Larry Lewallen and Ron Forbes had started their own inspections company called National Insurance Inspections. Norma Ruiz and Jeremy Davis were working for National. Some other Allied employees began migrating to National.

Things got crazy when Allied filed a lawsuit against National. Allied was alleging that Larry Lewallen and Ron Forbes were using proprietary information that belonged to Allied. I was considering moving to National at the time because things at Allied seemed to be going off kilter, but I changed my mind after the lawsuit was filed.

Even though some things at Allied seemed to be moving in a positive direction, there were some dark clouds developing. Allied started to lose major accounts such as CSAA. Victoria Riddle probably didn't help matters when she sent out a Christmas email to the clients about her personal religious philosophy.

Much to my dismay, I was being assigned Millennium reports again. I talked to Perry Riddle and told him I had problems with Millennium and I got moved to an account called Arrowhead.

Perry and Victoria Riddle decided they wanted to move Allied into doing commercial inspections. No one at Allied had any background doing commercial inspections. They approached me about possibly reviewing the new commercial lines. But part of the process involved taking road trips to talk to insurance company representatives. I told Perry Riddle that I couldn't physically take road trips and I'm sure he didn't like that much.

My new supervisor was named Alexis King. I didn't come in with any preconceived ideas about Alexis. But it bothered me that I (and other people) started to get extremely discourteous emails from her.

One day I got an email from her that irked me and I emailed her back that I was tired of getting nasty emails. Victoria Riddle thought that was "disrespectful" and told me she was "ending our business relationship." I thought and still think that it was a gross overreaction. If anyone had shown "disrespect," it was Alexis.

**NATIONAL INSURANCE
INSPECTIONS SERVICES**

I had already been talking to Larry Lewallen about possibly moving over to National. He sounded personable when I talked to him and I deluded myself that maybe I had been wrong about him when he was at Allied. I thought maybe it was his mother, Jan Sharp, who was most responsible for the oppressive conditions at Allied.

I went to an interview with Larry Lewallen and his wife Debra on a rainy February day. I was impressed by the office. It was mostly empty when I got there. A few desks were scattered here and there for the first few people who started working at National.

Whoever designed the building liked mirrors. There were mirrors in the elevators and so many mirrors in the restroom it was like a carnival funhouse.

The view was impressive. I could see Herndon Avenue through the big picture windows. A balcony ran outside the office. The break room was small, but I didn't use the break room anyway.

In the interview we talked some about Allied Inspections. Larry Lewallen's opinion was that his mother and stepfather, Jan and Don Sharp, weren't willing to cut their salaries (reportedly $40,000 a month for each of them) to free up money to invest in the business. He said the suit Allied filed against him was mostly an attempt to hurt him financially.

He didn't have kind words for his sister, Victoria Riddle. He alleged that she had stolen his "forms" in a previous business endeavor. He said that he was strongly opposed to Victoria being moved into a management position at Allied. One day he found his company credit cards had been canceled and it was evident he was being forced out at Allied.

I didn't expect to start work for a while until business picked up, but I got a call a few days later from Norma Leyva, formerly Norma Ruiz. She was the office manager. A woman named Raquel Salazar, who had worked at Allied as a reviewer, was the reviewer supervisor. Raquel was apparently a favorite of Debra Lewallen.

When I first started there wasn't a desk available, so I worked in the conference room. I started off with the dreaded paper reports and I discovered that the inspectors working for National were no better than the inspectors working for Allied Inspections. I also discovered that Raquel really enjoyed the power she had as a supervisor.

I didn't know Raquel all that well when she worked at Allied as a reviewer. I know that one woman there used to call Raquel "Shorty." Raquel is short and I've wondered if she had a chip on her shoulder. She also was a mother at a young age and wasn't very formally educated.

The management at National also had an obsession about language. For example, the word "risk" is used in the inspections business to describe the property being insured. We couldn't use the word "risk." We had to use the word "home." We had referred to inspectors as "inspectors" at Allied, but at National they became "field reps." Later on, we were forbidden to use the words "debris" or "clutter." We were also not supposed to use the word "about" when indicating something was being estimated.

I moved from the conference room to the mail room until new desks arrived and were assembled. Then I was assigned to a desk not far from the office Larry and Debra Lewallen shared. A guy named Gino sat behind me.

I could hear Gino frequently dropping the "F" word and furiously scrolling down the web page with his computer mouse. National had designed their web site to have one long page instead of multiple pages with links. I personally found the National design cumbersome.

I could hear Larry Lewallen and especially Debra Lewallen on the phone all day recruiting inspectors. Debra Lewallen liked to talk about her own experience of being an inspector. They used a variety of media to recruit inspectors, including Craigslist. I've never been able to get a straight answer about what qualifications, if any, a prospective inspector must have. It seemed to me that it was mostly having a digital camera and a warm body.

Inspectors also got very little training. They were thrown into a situation where they had to find their own way and the reviewers paid the price. One woman inspector from New York submitted diagrams that were absolutely unusable. Inspectors, in general, never seemed to understand configurations such as bi-level or tri-level homes, or the importance of square footage.

The biggest problem, among many problems, I had with reports was when an inspector said he or she measured the house and the square footage differed substantially from what we were told it should be. Most of the time it was because the inspector simply didn't measure correctly. We would wind up adjusting the diagram to try to get the diagram square footage within 10% of what we wanted.

When I was at Allied Inspections one inspector even said he couldn't draw the second level of a home on the diagram because he couldn't go inside the home and measure it from the inside. That was simply absurd. The same inspector said he couldn't verify fire hydrant distances because he couldn't drive around the neighborhood to check. You found yourself wanting to throw up your hands.

To be fair, inspectors are expected to possess a pretty impressive set of skills.

They have to map out their inspection schedule so they aren't bouncing around everywhere. They have to deal with the home's occupants, who can sometimes be extremely unfriendly. They have to deal with bad weather and vicious dogs. They have to deal with houses that sometimes have bizarre shapes or features. Then they have to complete the forms from the inspection company, download their photos, draw the diagram, and, theoretically, write notes about what they saw. Most inspectors don't do their jobs well.

The fees are fairly small for inspectors too, which probably inspires questionable behavior. Occasionally, you saw a car mirror in the photos, which indicated the inspector didn't even get out of his car to look at the house. They zoomed in with their cameras, snapped photos, and moved on. Even when mirrors weren't visible, I strongly suspected some inspectors were just taking photos from far away.

Another thing I noticed was that inspectors have their "pet" answers for questions. It's always the same kind of siding or roofing. A slope is always the same number of degrees. A fire hydrant is never visible. And so on. Inspectors probably don't even check, but just give a stock answer to the questions.

The "pet" answer problem has become more significant because some of the new replacement cost programs are very exacting. The creators of a program called 360 Value brag that their program calculates the replacement cost down to the "last nail" in the home.

Most inspectors I dealt with either didn't know what 360 Value required, or probably didn't care. For example, 360 Value wanted even uncovered patio slabs included to calculate the replacement cost. Inspectors rarely included patio slabs . It was difficult enough to get even basics like open porches included.

Another problem with 360 Value and inspection reports in general is the vast amount of minutiae. You get into debates about whether an area is a patio or a porch or a lattice roof or fiberglass and on and on. I have a hard time believing it makes much difference in the scheme of things.

I wasn't at National long before I started to see the micromanaging style that would characterize the place. I had to see Norma one morning in her office about my "totals." "Totals" was a recurring theme. Management decided you had to do a certain number of reports, come hell or high water, and when you didn't meet that arbitrary goal you got hassled. It didn't matter if you got reports from hell; you were just supposed to generate those "numbers."

I had heard good things about Debra Lewallen. But what I heard wasn't correct. I didn't like Debra Lewallen.

After my friends Melody and Bev started working at National we all got an email one day that Debra wanted to meet with us in the conference room. When we met it was another complaint about "totals." She told us, "I don't know what they did to you over at Allied." In essence, we were told we were too cautious. There was a certain irony to that since I got hassled over relatively minor errors a good deal of my time at National.

If you even hinted that working at National was as bad or maybe worse than Allied Inspections, you set off considerable outrage with Debra Lewallen and Norma Leyva. It was a little like going to the Vatican and yelling "God is dead!" (Hint: it was worse at National)

Early in my time at National they lured an account away from Allied Inspections. The company is called Arrowhead and Arrowhead requested inspections from all over the country. It might have been the biggest account Allied had at that point and losing it started their eventual demise.

I worked on lots of Arrowhead reports down through the years and it seemed to me that their underwriters became more like Millennium underwriters all the time.

I inadvertently transposed a couple of numbers on two replacement costs and it was suddenly a *cause celebre.* I had to meet with Raquel Salazar in the conference room and I was told that Larry "was upset." I was astonished. I told Raquel that I wasn't perfect. I realized then that Raquel was a pretend supervisor. She was more an enforcer for Larry and Debra Lewallen.

I once told Norma Leyva that it seemed all I ever heard was a constant stream of negativity, but she didn't respond.

On another morning I got an email from Norma Leyva again complaining about "totals." It turned out that Bev and Melody both got the same email. I went to Larry Lewallen's office and asked if I could speak to him.

He admitted that he told Norma to send the email. He went into an explanation about the cost of running a business such as leasing the office and all the rest, and said if he couldn't make a profit there was no point in being in business. I didn't disagree with any of that.

But he suggested that somehow my "totals" weren't as high as he wanted because I wasn't properly motivated. "I bet if I paid you $2.80 a report you would find a way to get your totals up," he told me. Interestingly enough, when I worked at home and got paid $2.80 a report my production was about the same as it had been in the office.

He also made some disparaging comments about writers. I let it go, but I was thinking, "People have heard of

William Shakespeare. How many businessmen do you remember from that time?"

I was furious. The Lewallen duo must have talked and thought they had gone too far because they asked Bev, Melody, and me to meet with them that afternoon.

Things didn't really change except possibly for the worse. They emulated Allied Inspections in creating "teams." Team members were assigned to a supervisor, who in turn was subordinate to Raquel Salazar and to Norma Leyva. Gino, the young guy who sat behind me, was named as my supervisor.

I got occasional emails from Raquel Salazar about errors. Her emails would begin like an indictment: "On such and such a day you did a report and you did this." I thought the tone of her emails was rude and I mentioned it to Norma Leyva. Norma just couldn't see anything rude about Raquel's emails. I also resented the implication that I was supposed to sort through a mass of data, have stringent production requirements, and never make a mistake.

Gino wasn't a supervisor long before there was a major brouhaha. He met with Larry and Debra Lewallen. His brother, who had recently started at National, was also included in the meeting. There was yelling involved.

Gino came in the next morning and on his way out told another guy and me to "watch your backs."

It turned out that Gino and his brother had exchanged emails critical of management at National, including Norma Leyva. The emails went over National's server and management evidently read the emails. The Lewallens took great offense and fired Gino and his brother.

I inadvertently overheard a conversation Debra Lewallen had with someone at the Employment Development Department. She was doing her best to deny Gino unemployment benefits.

Then there were two bits of news. One was that National was expanding, but didn't have enough desks. They were hiring people to work at home. The other news was that they going to take on Millennium reports big time again. I decided to ask if I could work at home.

I approached Norma Leyva. She said that home workers had to work part time and without benefits, which was obviously a major drawback. Later on, though, she said Larry Lewallen was open to the idea. I could work for $2.80 a report and retain my benefits.

The question then was whether I could get high speed Internet service and if I could get Internet Explorer to work. I had been experiencing problems with

Internet Explorer and it was the only browser that would work with National's system.

Debra Lewallen approached me and rather testily asked if I could give them a decision. I found out I could get high speed Internet and I finally got Internet Explorer to work.

So I started working at home in December, 2009, and I found I needed to work seven days a week to make a living. I usually worked shorter days on Saturday and on Sunday. Working every day was preferable to working in their office.

Even though I was getting paid by the report, management wanted me to clock in and out.

One of the drawbacks of working at home for National Insurance Inspections was, in effect, being on call. Management was forever sending a list of priority reports that needed to be closed as quickly as possible. Sometimes I would get several hours of priority reports after I had already worked eight or more hours.

One day Raquel Salazar sent some priority reports and I clocked out to take a break because I had been working for something like eight hours without a break. Then I got an abrasive email that she had to reassign the reports because I had clocked out.

But being snotty was Raquel's *modus operandi* for everyone except for the sycophants in the office.

After I worked at home a while, management decided we needed to have staff meetings in the office about twice a month. I objected because I wanted no part of going into their office and because it seemed to me almost everything discussed could be covered in either emails or phone calls.

When I went to one meeting I had to talk to Norma Leyva and Debra Lewallen about an email exchange with Raquel Salazar. I was getting harassing emails about "totals" and I finally told Raquel there was no point in flogging me for production. Norma Leyva and Debra Lewallen took great offense at my use of the word "flogging."

In June, 2010, something happened to my Internet connection. I tried for a day or two to get it working again, including getting a new modem, but my provider finally said a technician would have to come out. Norma Leyva called and wanted me to work in the office a couple of days until my Internet connection was repaired.

On my second day there Debra Lewallen ordered a staff meeting in the conference room. Lots of us were lined up against the wall because there weren't enough chairs. It had the setting of an execution.

She sat at the conference table and began, "You probably noticed so-and-so leaving. We had to fire her because she made a mistake that cost us an account."

She had a paper report that I suppose was the cause of all the drama. I didn't see the report. It sounded like the controversy had something to do with the diagram.

Then Debra Lewallen went into a tirade, "We've worked hard to build this company and we aren't going to let people mess it up," or something to that effect. The gist of her tirade was that we, the employees, were scum and that management was much put upon. I wished at the time I could record her display and put it on YouTube. She also used a phrase that has become repellent to me, "We're good people!" That was the last day I worked in the office at National Insurance Inspections.

I switched my schedule at home to working graveyard shift. I have tended to be a night owl anyway. But I was tired of getting inundated with priority reports that I was somehow miraculously supposed to finish. I felt that working graveyard hours gave management less opportunity to exploit me.

After several months of getting paid by the report Norma Leyva told me that management decided everyone would work as hourly employees. The good news was that I would get a little more time off (when there weren't mandatory overtime requirements). The bad news was that I was under their performance standards for "numbers" again. They would arbitrarily decide you should complete a certain number of reports per hour and if you didn't meet that standard you got hassled. At first it was three reports an hour.

I began to dread any email that had Raquel Salazar's name on it. It was invariably something negative. It was a complaint about a mistake on a report. It was a complaint about "totals." It was a demand for more hours or working hours I normally didn't work. I began to think of her as the "Little Nazi."

In the summer of 2011 I got a call from Norma Leyva. National had lost some of its Millennium account business and they were cutting my hours. I was down to 29 hours a week and I didn't have benefits any longer. One of the benefits I lost was health insurance, which became significant a few months later.

A schedule at National Insurance Inspections really didn't mean much. When my hours were cut I was told I would work eight hours on Monday, Tuesday, and Wednesday. I would have Wednesday night off and then work five hours on Friday.

But suddenly management wanted 40 hours a week from me, even though I still didn't receive any benefits. After a stint of working full time hours I asked Norma Leyva if I would get credit toward any benefits, such as vacation time, and the answer was no.

As if the job didn't have enough pressure, management introduced a new wrinkle called "review issues." The supervisors spot checked reports and sent us emails about so-called "review issues." Early on, the emails I got were about things I had never even been informed about. For example, on the 360 Value reports there was a distinction in things like architectural roof shingles or composition roof shingles, or in clapboard siding and plywood, and so on.

What bothered me most about the "review issue" procedure was that it was arbitrary. A number of things in the inspections business are matters of opinion, but a "review issue" was treated like an error. Another issue that bothered me was that some errors were so incredibly minor they could be fixed by the supervisor in seconds, but we had to go through an entire asinine procedure of having the email sent to us, looking up the report, making the change, and emailing the supervisor. For a company so intent on production, it was very counterproductive.

I learned that I could expect an email about 1:30 every afternoon about some "review issue." I started to question almost everything I did on reports because it might show up as a "review issue." What little morale I had was destroyed.

Late in 2011 I noticed what looked like a rash on my right leg. It went away after a few days, but then a much more severe rash developed on both legs. My legs and feet were swollen so badly I could barely wear shoes. My legs were also draining an incredible amount of fluid.

I resisted going to the doctor because I didn't have health insurance. But my condition was worsening and the pain was constant. I went to a clinic in May, 2012, to get checked out and they admitted me to Fresno Community Hospital.

When I was in the Emergency Room I got diagnosed with an irregular heartbeat. I asked for something to help mitigate the pain in my legs. The nurse gave me morphine and it didn't even help much at first. I remember a guy asking me if I could put down a deposit for my time in the E. R and I put $500 on a credit card.

I was in the E. R. overnight and then assigned to a room. I had the luxury of having the room to myself. The nurses and doctors who came to visit me wore yellow hazards materials suits in the event I had something infectious and, I suppose, to avoid transmitting anything infectious to me.

I had a heart monitor attached to my chest and an IV attached to my arm. I had problems keeping the leads from the heart monitor attached because they came loose when I had to move.

After a few days I was discharged and I asked for a week away from work, even though it would be unpaid. I needed some time to heal. But a few days later a home health care nurse detected my heart was beating at 140 beats per minute, about twice the normal rate, and I was taken by ambulance again to the Emergency Room at Fresno Community Hospital.

I spent a night that seemed like an eternity in the E. R. hooked up to an IV and a heart monitor. I was on a gurney in a hallway. I had to undergo an ultrasound that was pretty painful. I got very little sleep because the lights are always on in the E. R. and it's noisy. People are talking and monitors are beeping. Lab technicians also come around constantly to draw blood. I told one lab technician that Dracula had nothing on them.

A wound specialist came around and applied a silver nitrate covering to the open sores on my legs and it burned the way I would imagine a blow torch would feel. It is apparently very effective at killing bacteria.

I didn't have anything to eat for over 24 hours and when I was finally transferred to a room a nurse gave me a cheeseburger. It may have been the most delicious meal in my life.

I didn't get a call or even a get well card from the management at National Insurance Inspections during either hospital stay, even though I made them aware I was in the hospital.

After I was discharged a second time I had to deal with the financial monster created by the hospital visits. I got a bill from the ambulance company for close to $900 for a trip across the street from the clinic to the E. R. The hospital stays averaged over $20,000 each. There were a host of other charges.

I was informed about a program called MISP, but I quickly got shot down for MISP. I had too much money in my checking account, they said. Then an advocate at Fresno Community Hospital began working with me on an application for Medi-Cal. If I got Medi-Cal, my hospital and other expenses would be paid. If not, I would probably be facing bankruptcy.

As I began dealing with the swelling in my legs, my doctors and nurses said I needed to elevate my legs. Having them flat on the floor, such as I had to do when working on the computer, was really bad for them. I finally asked my doctor if he would recommend limiting my hours and he wrote a prescription to limit my hours to the 29 hours a week the National management had previously mandated. Actually, he would have preferred I work fewer hours, but I told him I needed the 29 hours to survive.

Raquel Salazar wanted a copy of my doctor's note, so I made a photocopy and sent it to her.

Raquel introduced another aspect to her micromanaging style. I called it "intercepting" a report. Part of our procedure was to return reports to inspectors if we had a question. I tried not to send reports back unless it was a major issue and I couldn't see what I needed in the photos. For example, if a swimming pool was unfenced, it was a major condition and sometimes I couldn't tell from the photos if the pool was fenced.

Raquel would put the report back in the queue and then make a condescending comment about how the pool (or whatever) was fenced. So I felt caught in a Catch-22. If I sent reports back for a legitimate question, Raquel interfered. If I made the call on my own and the client company complained, then I would get an email about the company complaining.

Then management raised the bar again. They expected us to complete four reports an hour, even with detailed 360 Value reports. I knew that four reports an hour was totally unrealistic, but I got Raquel's charming emails about "totals" every week. Then they told me that some people in the office were meeting their four report an hour quota.

One day I called Raquel and asked if I could to talk to someone who was meeting their four an hour quota. Of course, I never got a response.

Things continued about the same. My frustration was boiling over. Then I got another email from Raquel complaining about a wood stove item that was checked on a report, but with no interview to verify the wood stove. It was an Arrowhead report. The item was probably marked by the inspector and it was one of those items that I normally didn't give much attention in my quest for "numbers."

So I answered her email and said I couldn't go back in time to change the history of the report. I never understood the reason she sent me emails over picayune complaints by the company because I couldn't undo whatever caused their complaint.

I also asked if she had ever considered a job satisfaction survey. I know they never asked for my feedback. Then I said I had some grievances against management that I wasn't going to detail. I'll mention some of them here.

The biggest grievance was the incessant demands for production when not much was done to aid me in doing more production. I wrote one of their supervisors a detailed email about problems with the website. Their website was filled with items that required redundant entries and other items that should have had some kind of computer prompt requiring the inspector to complete the information. A prompt would have prevented my apparently "horrible" error about the wood stove pipe, for instance.

I also resented the whole "review issue" mess. I never knew exactly what their procedure was supposed to accomplish. If it was meant to destroy morale, it succeeded admirably.

The constant micromanaging by Raquel was another issue. I didn't really feel I could do my job anymore because she would find some way to interfere.

Another consistent problem at National Inspections was Larry Lewallen's penchant for constantly adding new work while expecting production levels to remain the same or even increase.

For example, if the home was part of a townhouse complex, we had to tell the insurance company how many units were attached. The inspectors rarely provided that information, so the option was to look at the satellite photo and more or less take a guess.

If a swimming pool had a ladder, we were supposed to tell the insurance company if the ladder was a locking ladder. Again, it was information that would rarely be provided by the inspector.

If the home was located in an area with brush and the inspector didn't complete the brush report, I had to complete the report. But the inspector got paid for the report they didn't even do.

The list just went on and on.

I took an unpaid sick night off after the exchange with Raquel Salazar because I didn't feel well and because I was angry. Then the next two days I wasn't assigned any work and there was no explanation. I suspected I was being "punished."

I contacted a labor attorney to get advice about what I should do. They could have kept me in limbo indefinitely, technically keeping me on the payroll, but not assigning any work. The labor attorney's advice was to go ahead and file for unemployment. If National began assigning me work again, I would simply report that to the Employment Development Department.

After I sent my email to Raquel Salazar, I got a typically sanctimonious email from Norma Leyva. Debra was "upset" by my email (the Lewallens get upset a lot). She thought the "tone" of my email was bad and so on. Then she brought up Allied Inspections indirectly.

She said that Larry and Debra Lewallen had built up National Inspections and how it was better than the company we had previously worked for (it wasn't).

On the morning of January 7, 2013, I worked overnight the way I had been doing for months. I even spent an hour of my own time auditing reports to find any errors I could correct. After I clocked out, I dozed off.

I was awakened when my cell phone rang. At first I thought it might be my home health care nurse. Then the caller identified herself as Debra and she quickly said she was going to have to "let me go." Then she went into an incredible rant.

From her rant, you would think I was the worst human to walk the planet. She started reading parts of my email back to me (as though I didn't know what I said) and threw in the old homily about how they were "good people."

She said my suggestion about a job satisfaction survey was an "insult."

She said something about how I didn't like Raquel (I didn't know liking Raquel was a part of the job description.)

You would think, from what she said, that they had done me a terrific favor letting me work at home. Never mind that I probably worked harder at home than I had worked in the office (which was pretty hard). I gave them lots of free time off the clock in an effort to meet their production quotas and I also gave them free time when I audited my reports.

I don't know if she would have ever shut up except that my prepaid cell phone minutes ran out. In retrospect, I wish I had simply hung up on her.

I think the evidence strongly suggests that she and her husband are not "good people." They are rapacious and ruthless business people who treat their employees as disposable commodities. But none of that tempers their incredible self-righteousness.

CONCLUSION

National Insurance Inspections is a paradigm of what is wrong with the economy in the United States. Workers, particularly since the Reagan administration, have lost more and more power. The Reagan administration attacked unions when Reagan fired the air traffic controllers. The National Labor Relations Board, which is supposed to look out for the interest of workers, was strongly pro-business. We have seen a proliferation of "at will" employment, which strongly favors employers over employees.

Congressional Republicans are now pushing legislation that would effectively do away with overtime. They would like to replace overtime with "comp time." The employee would supposedly get compensated with time off rather than money. I'm sure Larry and Debra Lewallen would relish that. Mandatory overtime has been a staple of their management style for years. Without the constraints of overtime law I can see them and others like them radically abusing their employees.

We tend to think of history as linear. We like to think the human race has progressed, but I think there is a definite regressive movement now. Union members fought and in some cases died to win rights such as paid sick leave, paid vacations, and overtime pay and increasingly we see attacks on what we thought were basic rights.

Sweatshops are usually envisioned as dark dingy factories, but offices are increasingly becoming sweatshops. The forty hour week is becoming an anachronism. A few years ago when you left your job at the end of the day it was over until the next work day. Now, with the advent of new technology, you're never really away from your job. You have to check your email or your text messages or you get a call on your cell phone.

Privacy doesn't exist anymore. You are under constant surveillance. People complain about government surveillance, but private industry is probably an even bigger offender. You get "profiled" as a consumer so you can be targeted for ads that supposedly fit your interests. You are on surveillance cameras at many businesses you visit. Employers read your emails and they have power akin to the slave masters of past times. There may not be literal "flogging" these days, but metaphorical flogging is a constant reality.

But even as conditions get worse, we're told that we have the best economic system in the world. We're told that if you aren't successful in the United States it's your fault. The business interests in the United States have the greatest propaganda apparatus ever assembled. They own powerful advertising firms, they use well-refined public relations techniques, and even the so-called objective news media are tools for business interests.

This is just one person's history of dealing with the reality of working in the United States economy and I suspect my story is fairly common. Let us celebrate working people and the contributions of working people and not be manipulated by the people who exploit us and then throw us away like yesterday's newspaper.